TO

_____

FROM

_____

DATE

_____

Resting in Jesus

A 30-Day Walk with Mary and Martha

DEVOTIONAL GUIDE

—

APRIL RODGERS

DaySpring
LIVE YOUR FAITH

INTRODUCTION

HELLO, FRIEND!

It's wonderful to meet you here among the pages of *Resting in Jesus*. I wonder if I could ask you a personal question right off the bat. Is there anything you are facing today that is causing you to be weary or worried? Is it final exams, a job with a glass ceiling, an unfaithful spouse, unresolved family dynamics, a health concern or diagnosis, a wayward child, or an aging parent? Or perhaps you aren't facing any difficulties in this season of your life, but the thought of resting in Jesus sounds like exactly what you need. Whatever it is that brought you to this devotional guide, please know that I am delighted you are here.

Over the next thirty days (or six weeks, however long your walk takes), we are going to take each step with purpose, turning our faces toward the sun and feeling the cool breeze around us. As we put one foot in front of the other, keeping Christ as our focus, we will discover what deep truths were revealed over two thousand years ago to two sisters of Bethany by the names of Mary and Martha.

Within the pages of Scripture, we find these two sisters. One with a thirst for knowledge and one with the gift of hospitality. One with a quiet strength and one with a take-charge personality. One with a desire to worship and one with a declaration of belief. Each with their own set of strengths and weaknesses but both with a heart for Jesus.

Mary and Martha have much to teach us about resting in Jesus. As we walk alongside these sisters over the next few weeks, we're going to get up close and personal with their stories. We'll see that they experienced heartache, loss, comparison, frustration, and deep disappointment. But they also experienced inclusion, affirmation, revelation, and even resurrection because of their close proximity and relationship with Jesus. Through the examples of these two sisters, we find that true rest has more to do with our ability to trust and believe in Jesus than it does with living a carefree life.

This life is filled with things that weigh us down—some by our own doing and some by circumstances beyond our control. But the advantage we have as Christ followers is that we can find rest and possess hope even when life hands us challenges. The secret we are privy to is that we serve a God who can handle our doubts and fears, and He is trustworthy. Even in the midst of our trials, we can obtain rest—not in our own strength, because that will fail us over time. We find rest because of who we are in Jesus.

Jesus said that *if* we come to Him, He will give us rest. And not just any kind of rest but deep, soul rest. The key is that we must come to Him first. He must be a part of our lives if we want to rest in Him. Mary and Martha were known for opening their hearts and home to Jesus. They cultivated a friendship that resulted in a deep love for Him. They broke bread together. Wept together. Walked the same roads together. Now it's our turn.

If we truly want rest, the best thing we can do is walk with the One who created us. So, let's take a walk. Let's take a walk that allows us to leave our anxiety and worry behind and moves us forward in confident hope. Let's take a walk that will ultimately leave us better than when we first began.

Are you ready? Me too! Let's start resting in Jesus as we keep in step with Mary, Martha, and the Master.

TO HIM BE THE GLORY,
April Rodgers

Scan for a downloadable leader's guide and for more encouragement from April

WELCOMING JESUS INTO YOUR HEART AND HOME

While they were traveling, He entered a village, and a woman named Martha welcomed Him into her home. LUKE 10:38 CSB

Don't you just love a good dinner party? After a warm invitation is extended and accepted, it's time to pick out the menu and straighten up the home—fluff the pillows, sweep the floor, and set the table. Whether the meal is homemade or catered, it doesn't matter. Because the most important part of the evening is simply when friends gather around the table and allow the conversation and laughter to flow as the night progresses. Eventually, goodbyes are said at the door with promises to do it again soon. And even though we are left with a kitchen full of dirty dishes, we typically find that after opening our homes to others, our hearts are just as full as our stomachs.

Martha must have felt the same way when the time came for her to bid farewell to her cherished guests. As the head of the house that she shared with Mary and Lazarus, her sister and brother, Martha was certainly known for her hospitality in the village of Bethany. She was very much in charge and was willing to receive guests into her home, even if her guest of honor came traveling with a clan of twelve other men.

The gospel of Luke records that Martha *welcomed* Jesus into her home. She didn't begrudgingly open the door for Him and His disciples. No. She wanted His presence to fill her home, and thus she swung wide open the door to host Him. As Jesus placed one holy foot and then another onto her property, did Martha feel the atmosphere shift? Could she feel the peace that only He provides permeate her home? Can you imagine what it must have felt like to welcome the Son of God into your home for a dinner party? I bet she never wanted to say goodbye to this special guest.

Perhaps the first time Martha opened her door to Jesus, she was curious to see if He truly was the Son of God, and perhaps you are wondering the same thing today.

In Revelation 3:20 (NLT), Jesus said, *"Look! I stand at the door and knock. If you hear My voice and open the door, I will come in, and we will share a meal together as friends."* Jesus gives each one of us the same invitation. He stands at the door of our hearts and knocks, but it's up to us whether or not we open the door and welcome Him into our lives.

He will not force Himself through the door, but oh, how He wants to have dinner with us! He, too, loves a good dinner party and wants to bring His peace and salvation as He comes to reside and rest in our hearts. But the question is, will we let Him in? It's only when we wholeheartedly welcome Him into our day-to-day routines that we will truly find rest.

Reflection
- QUESTIONS -

What expectations do you come with in regard to this devotional guide? What do you hope to have achieved once it's finished?

_____

_____

_____

_____

_____

_____

_____

_____

_____

_____

_____

_____

_____

_____

_____

_____

_____

_____

_____

_____

Is Jesus knocking at the door of your heart? If you're honest with yourself, have you let Him all the way in? Even into your messy kitchen? List anything that is holding you back from opening your heart to Him all the way.

_____

_____

_____

_____

_____

_____

_____

_____

_____

Take a moment right now to welcome God into the deepest crevices of your heart and home. Feel His perfect peace surround you, and record your response to His presence below.

_____

_____

_____

_____

_____

_____

_____

_____

_____

SCRIPTURE

"Look! I stand at the door and knock. If you hear My voice and open the door, I will come in, and we will share a meal together as friends."

REVELATION 3:20 NLT

There is no one else who has the power to save us, for there is only one name to whom God has given authority by which we must experience salvation: the name of Jesus.

ACTS 4:12 TPT

The Lord now chose seventy-two other disciples and sent them ahead in pairs to all the towns and places He planned to visit. These were His instructions to them: "The harvest is great, but the workers are few. So pray to the Lord who is in charge of the harvest; ask Him to send more workers into his fields. Now go, and remember that I am sending you out as lambs among wolves. Don't take any money with you, nor a traveler's bag, nor an extra pair of sandals. And don't stop to greet anyone on the road.
"Whenever you enter someone's home, first say, 'May God's peace be on this house.' If those who live there are peaceful, the blessing will stand; if they are not, the blessing will return to you. Don't move around from home to home. Stay in one place, eating and drinking what they provide. Don't hesitate to accept hospitality, because those who work deserve their pay."

LUKE 10:1–7 NLT

PRAYER

Jesus, what a privilege it is to take this walk of faith with You. I ask You to come and meet me as I commit to walk alongside Mary, Martha, and You. Reveal to me things that are keeping me from resting in You, and make known to me anything that is hindering Your peace from resting on me. I give You permission to come into every aspect of my life. I open the door of my heart fully to You—even the messy parts that I would rather remain hidden. Teach me to embrace a lifestyle that is authentic and transparent, knowing that with You I can be the best version of myself if I am willing to let You in. Today I resolve to hold nothing back, knowing that You didn't hold anything back from me whenever You came to die for my sins. I declare that You are the Son of God, and it is my greatest delight to have You in my heart and home. There is nothing better than having dinner with You as my Savior and Friend. You are so very welcome in this place. Amen.

Moment to Breathe

Take a moment to breathe in God's rest and exhale out your tiredness. Imagine that you are at the beach. The water is blue, and the breeze is just right—not too strong and not too chilly. You are grateful for the getaway because your life has been hectic lately, and you can't wait to rest and relax in the sun. But as you make your way to the shoreline, there are throngs of people. Sand is flying, and babies are crying. This is not the refreshment you had desired. You wanted peace and quiet and rest for your weary soul, but now your high expectations are dissolving into the wind like sunscreen from an aerosol bottle. Now imagine that Jesus is toward the east. The sun is illuminating Him, and He is beckoning you to walk toward Him. You take a step and then another, and as you do, you feel your anxiety begin to decrease. It's not that the distractions and dangers of being at the beach aren't still there; it's just that your focus has changed and you are walking toward your rest with purpose. So, take a deep breath in and receive your invitation.

You will keep in perfect peace those whose minds are steadfast, because they trust in You.
ISAIAH 26:3 NIV

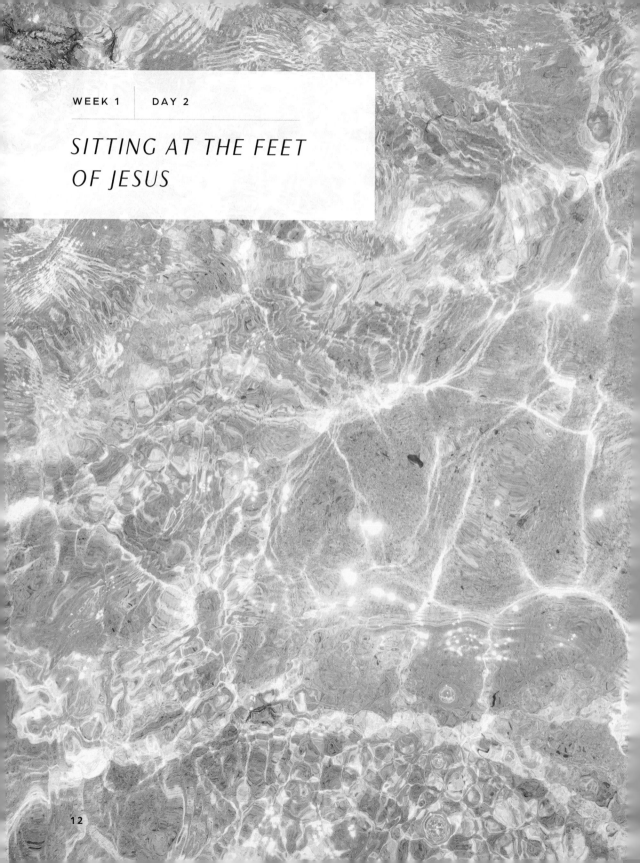

SITTING AT THE FEET OF JESUS

She had a sister named Mary, who also sat at the Lord's feet and was listening to what He said.
LUKE 10:39 CSB

Now that we have had a chance to fully invite Jesus into all the places in our hearts and homes, let's grab ourselves a cup of coffee or our favorite energy drink and make our way to the living room. Jesus is there, and He is just about to start teaching.

In the times of Mary and Martha, a rabbi (teacher) would have many disciples. When he was ready to teach them a spiritual lesson, he would sit down, and his disciples would sit all around him—thus the phrase "sitting at the feet" of one's rabbi. It was normal to see these pockets of people all around the land of Israel. But what was not normal was to see a woman among them. Women were not typically included in such circles.

However, that is precisely where we find Mary—sitting at the feet of her Rabbi, soaking in every word. Did she have to fight for a spot, politely elbowing her way through the men so she could get close enough to Jesus to hear His teaching? Or perhaps she was personally welcomed by Jesus to take a seat with the disciples. Had she heard Jesus's teachings before and that's why she was willing to drop everything and sit at His feet, even at the expense of upsetting Martha? Whatever the circumstance, it seemed as if she realized this was her opportunity to learn from the very One who embodied wisdom and she was not about to let it pass her by.

If we want to be like Mary, we must be willing to press pause on our list of daily responsibilities and learn to simply sit down and quiet our hearts and minds. Which means that we've got to dig into God's Word for ourselves and spend time in prayer. We can also further our faith journey by walking alongside others who can teach us how to follow Jesus in the good seasons and the bad. Proverbs 13:20 says that those who walk with the wise will become wise. To glean from a spiritual mentor who has a deep and intimate relationship with Jesus is one way we can grow in wisdom, but absolutely nothing compares to sitting one-on-one with Jesus ourselves.

Mary's boldness to take her seat among Jesus's followers is empowering for us as women in today's day and age. He is worth putting aside the day-to-day grind and focusing on. The benefits are truly life-changing.

Reflection
- QUESTIONS -

Describe a time when you found yourself in a situation similar to Mary's, when despite knowing there were numerous tasks or responsibilities awaiting you, you were irresistibly drawn to spend time at the feet of Jesus. Reflect on the feelings and thoughts that arose during that moment, and share how it impacted your perspective or priorities.

Have you ever had a spiritual mentor who knew Jesus on a deep and intimate level? Write their name below. What have you gleaned by walking alongside that person?

_____

_____

_____

_____

_____

_____

_____

_____

_____

_____

In the book of Proverbs, wisdom is personified as a woman. Taking that into consideration, along with the fact that Mary was allowed to sit at the feet of her Rabbi, it's evident that Jesus affirms that women are invited to learn the deep things of God. With that in mind, take a moment to sit still in Jesus's presence and record here any wisdom that is revealed to you.

_____

_____

_____

_____

_____

_____

SCRIPTURE

The one who walks with the wise will become wise, but a companion of fools will suffer harm.

PROVERBS 13:20 CSB

Do not forsake wisdom, and she will protect you; love her, and she will watch over you.

PROVERBS 4:6 NIV

Therefore, let us approach the throne of grace with boldness, so that we may receive mercy and find grace to help us in time of need.

HEBREWS 4:16 CSB

Now a Jew named Apollos, an Alexandrian by birth, an eloquent man, came to Ephesus; and he was mighty in the Scriptures. This man had been instructed in the way of the Lord; and being fervent in spirit, he was speaking and teaching accurately the things concerning Jesus, being acquainted only with the baptism of John; and he began to speak out boldly in the synagogue. But when Priscilla and Aquila heard him, they took him aside and explained to him the way of God more accurately.

ACTS 18:24–26 NASB1995

P R A Y E R

Jesus, I long to sit at Your feet just like Mary did. Thank You for creating a space for me. I offer up to You now any feelings of insecurity I may have about understanding You and Your Word. Help me to come boldly to the throne of grace so I can receive Your mercy in my time of need. I also ask that you clear my mind of all distractions as I meet with You. Sometimes I feel as if my to-do list is more pressing than my need to sit at Your feet, so I am asking for Your help to prioritize my time with You first. Meeting with You gives life to my bones and teaches me how to rest in You.

Lord, bring me the rest I am seeking, but also fill me with Your wisdom. I desire to be a woman who is known for her wisdom, and I know this wisdom comes first from You and second by surrounding myself with other mentors who are wise. Put these wise people in my path and create opportunities for me to invest this wisdom into others. Today I boldly take my spot at Your feet and declare that I want more of You and Your wisdom, Jesus. Amen.

Moment to Breathe

Take a moment to breathe in God's rest and exhale out your insecurity. Imagine a room that is buzzing with excitement as Jesus enters through the door. Suddenly, Jesus looks directly at you and invites you to sit down and listen to Him. He has so much to teach you—He is, after all, the ultimate Rabbi. You may have felt that you aren't worthy enough to sit with the others who surround Him, but He silences those feelings as He begins to speak straight to your soul. He says you are worthy, not by your own accord but because of who He is in you. He talks about wisdom and how He loves to freely give to those who seek it above all else. You know without a doubt that you need wisdom for the circumstances you are facing, so you listen all the more intently. And as you sit and soak in every word, you find that your heart rate begins to level out and nothing else matters except you and your Rabbi, who is before you. Take one more deep breath in and receive His wisdom.

By wisdom a house is built, and through understanding it is established; through knowledge its rooms are filled with rare and beautiful treasures. PROVERBS 24:3–4 NIV

EARS TO HEAR

Her sister, Mary, sat at the Lord's feet, listening to what He taught.
LUKE 10:39 NLT

In the previous entry, we found Mary sitting at the feet of Jesus, even though it was highly unusual for women to do so. But Scripture tells us that she didn't just sit; she also *listened* to what Jesus said.

One of the truisms of motherhood is that children can "hear" the words that are being spoken without truly "listening" to their mother. The telltale sign is a faraway look in their eyes while they monotonously nod as the mother speaks. They may have heard her words, but were they actually listening? The proof of active listening is found in the action that follows.

When Jesus told the Parable of the Sower, He asked that those who had ears to hear should both listen and understand. Why was this so important? It was because He was giving different scenarios on how the listener *responds* to hearing the Word of God. After a powerful message or good women's conference, do we make vows to spend more time in God's Word, only to find that time quickly choked out by the worries of the world? Do we allow the Word to be snatched up before it even takes root, or do we cultivate a place for it to grow deep within our souls? Are we truly listening to what God is saying and applying it to our everyday lives, or are we nodding our heads and letting it go in one ear and out the other? The choice is ours.

If we love Jesus, then we can't help but want to deepen our relationship with Him, and one way we grow in our relationship with Jesus is by reading His Word. God's Word tells us how to navigate our lives and how to respond to the needs in our loved ones' lives. When you truly love Jesus, you not only want to "hear" Him, but you also want to take the next step and live in a way that shares His love with others. That's what it means to truly listen.

As we come to Jesus seeking rest, what we find is that just as much as we desire His rest, He longs to give it to us, because that is how He operates. He also knows that as we keep coming to Him and trusting in Him, we will want to spend time in His Word because that's how He best communicates with us. Such is the beauty of having a two-sided relationship with the Almighty.

Mary sat the feet of Jesus and truly listened to the life-giving words He spoke. She wanted to be there, soaking in His teachings. I imagine that every sacred word that was spoken fell on the fertile soil of her heart. And long after Jesus had ascended to the Father, the seeds that had been planted produced a hundredfold crop. This is what it means to have ears to hear!

Reflection
- QUESTIONS -

Take a moment to think about why you want to read God's Word. What are you hoping to gain or learn from it?

Mary was content to sit at Jesus's feet, and because she did, it cultivated a relationship with Jesus as her Lord. We can cultivate a relationship with God by reading and applying His Word to our lives. List two specific ways you can hear God's Word today and apply to it in your everyday life.

_____

_____

_____

_____

_____

_____

_____

_____

_____

Write out one or two things that you are believing God for in either your life or the life of a loved one. Then look up one or two of God's promises in His Word and record them here.

_____

_____

_____

_____

_____

_____

_____

_____

SCRIPTURE

"Listen! A farmer went out to plant some seed. As he scattered it across his field, some of the seed fell on a footpath, and the birds came and ate it. Other seed fell on shallow soil with underlying rock. The seed sprouted quickly because the soil was shallow. But the plant soon wilted under the hot sun, and since it didn't have deep roots, it died. Other seed fell among thorns that grew up and choked out the tender plants so they produced no grain. Still other seeds fell on fertile soil, and they sprouted, grew, and produced a crop that was thirty, sixty, and even a hundred times as much as had been planted!" Then He said, "Anyone with ears to hear should listen and understand."

MARK 4:3–9 NLT

But don't just listen to God's word. You must do what it says. Otherwise, you are only fooling yourselves. For if you listen to the word and don't obey, it is like glancing at your face in a mirror. You see yourself, walk away, and forget what you look like. But if you look carefully into the perfect law that sets you free, and if you do what it says and don't forget what you heard, then God will bless you for doing it.

JAMES 1:22–25 NLT

"Remember My words with your whole being. Write them down and tie them to your hands as a sign; tie them on your foreheads to remind you. Teach them well to your children, talking about them when you sit at home and walk along the road, when you lie down and when you get up."

DEUTERONOMY 11:18–19 NCV

PRAYER

Lord, please give me a hunger for Your Word that only You can provide. I commit to open my Bible and read it, but I need for You to give me a supernatural love for it like only You can. Don't let it go in one ear and out the other, but rather allow it to resonate deep within my spirit. Let it fall on the fertile soil of my heart and soul so I can apply it to every facet of my life. Reveal to me any hard or compact places that need to be softened so I can receive Your Word. Jesus, I know for certain that Your Word gives life, and I desperately need it so I can know what You have to say about who I am in You. I also know that reading Your Word will help me relate to others better, and I want that for every relationship I'm currently in. Teach me how to allow it to take root deep within me so I can stand on Your promises in the things I am believing You for. Give me ears to hear and a heart to understand. I love You, Lord, and I am grateful for Your Word. Amen.

Moment to Breathe

Take a moment to breathe in God's rest and exhale out your preconceived notions about God and His Word. Imagine that you are sitting beside Mary in her home, and as Jesus is speaking, your ears are completely attentive and your mind can comprehend all the words that are coming out of His mouth. You are not confused, nor are you struggling to understand what He means. In fact, you not only understand what Jesus is saying, but you also know exactly what He wants you to do with it. There is no vagueness; there is only clarity. And as Jesus's voice continues to land on your ears, you find that it makes your love for Him grow. You don't ever want Him to stop speaking directly to you because it is giving life to your weary bones. You can now relate to how the psalmist must have felt when he said that God's law was his delight because you feel a closeness to Him that you haven't felt before. With that in mind, take a deep breath in and receive your love for His Word!

I long for your salvation, O LORD, and your law is my delight.
PSALM 119:174 ESV

SEIZE THE DAY

But Martha was distracted by her many tasks, and she came up and asked, "Lord, don't You care that my sister has left me to serve alone? So tell her to give me a hand." LUKE 10:40 CSB

You may have heard this age-old adage: "The days are long, but the years are short." It's effortless to quote these words if we are mature in age, but that young mom in the grocery store with one child in the front of the buggy and one tucked in the main part amid an array of groceries may not believe this to be true. For her, the days seem to stretch out to no end.

Seasons come and go, and it's easy to offer God our excuses of why we were too distracted to sit at His feet day in and day out. We promise things like:

Lord, when my kids start school, I will have more time for You.

Lord, when I get that promotion, I can stop working so hard and spend more time with You.

Lord, when I retire, I will have all the time in the world for You!

And on and on it goes. Ever been there, my friend?

The thing about life is that it happens at a rapid pace, and if we're not careful it can pass us by before we even know what happened. What a tragedy that would be! We must be intentional to seize our opportunities to sit with Jesus each and every day.

Luke 10:40 (CSB) says, *"But Martha was distracted by her many tasks."* We witnessed Mary taking the time to sit and listen to Jesus's words, but here Martha is distracted with her many tasks, even though the same opportunity to sit and listen presented itself to her as well. However, before we cast judgment on Martha, let it be noted that Jesus and His disciples were most likely keen on eating at some point that night, so Martha's contribution was very much needed. It wasn't that her hospitality wasn't necessary. It was just that she was pulled away from the *main thing*, which was Jesus and the words He was teaching in that moment.

How often do we do the exact same things in our lives? We get pulled away by the many tasks that need to be done, and before we know it, we have missed out on the very thing that will feed our souls. Tasks are important—the baby has to be changed, the dinner has to be made, the bills have to be paid, the elderly parent has to be cared for—but these things cannot take the place of real interaction with Jesus. We must set the alarm, put a time limit on social media, decline that offer to add another event to our calendars. . . if that's what it takes to put away the distractions. It may be contrary to our nature at first, but once we get in a rhythm of choosing Jesus over our tasks, that's when we will be diligent to seize the day.

Reflection
- QUESTIONS -

Mary and Martha were presented with the same opportunity to sit at Jesus's feet and listen to His teachings, yet only one sister chose to seize it. Knowing how precious an invitation it was to sit and listen to Jesus, how does this change your perspective on what was going on in Martha's mind? Do you think she would have chosen differently had she not been distracted? Why or why not?

Do you ever find yourself wanting to spend time with Jesus but distracted by your to-do list? Try writing down all the things that are keeping you occupied and asking Him to take them from your thoughts so you can concentrate on Him and His Word. What are some of your "time wasters" that you can eliminate from your day? Ask the Lord to help you release those and replace them with something better.

\
\
\
\
\
\
\
\

Do you have a specific time set aside in your day that you use to consistently meet with Jesus? Why or why not?

\
\
\
\
\
\
\
\

SCRIPTURE

Very early in the morning, while it was still dark, Jesus got up, left the house and went off to a solitary place, where He prayed.

MARK 1:35 NIV

Set your minds on things above, not on earthly things.

COLOSSIANS 3:2 NIV

"Do not store up for yourselves treasures on earth, where moths and vermin destroy, and where thieves break in and steal. But store up for yourselves treasures in heaven, where moths and vermin do not destroy, and where thieves do not break in and steal. For where your treasure is, there your heart will be also."

MATTHEW 6:19–21 NIV

PRAYER

Lord, You know this life is busy. Sometimes it feels as if I'm spinning my wheels and not getting anywhere, and other times it feels as if I'm moving at a breakneck speed. I long to slow down and be close to You, yet so often I am distracted by my ever-present to-do list. I know my tasks are necessary, but help me to make it a habit to carve out time for You first. Forgive me when I put my busy life ahead of You. You don't deserve that, and I'm sorry for being easily distracted by all the things that need to be done. Teach me how to make better use of my time so I can rest and recharge my spirit with You, knowing it will make me more productive in the long run. Give me grace to know how to handle those pressing situations that need my full attention, but then gently redirect me back to a dedicated and consistent time with You. Jesus, You are where my joy is found, not in the things of this world. I reach for You first and ask You to help me seize each and every day. Amen.

Moment to Breathe

Take a moment to breathe in God's rest and exhale out all your distractions. Imagine that you are grocery shopping with small children. As you walk through the aisles, you are trying to remember what all was on your list that you unfortunately left sitting on your kitchen counter. You only have a few minutes to get what you need before you have to be in the carpool line to pick up your eldest child. As you are distractedly throwing things in your buggy, your child points to a Man who is offering her a slice of an orange. She asks you if it's okay to take it from Him. You immediately recognize Him as Jesus because He has offered you this good fruit many times. You tell her it's fine to accept it as you hold out your hand to take a slice for yourself. As you taste its sweetness, you decide to keep in step with Him in a more intentional way and watch as things inevitably fall in line. As an added bonus, you find that the more time you spend in His presence, the more productive you are the rest of the day. Take another deep breath in and receive His sweet presence.

You make known to me the path of life; in your presence there is fullness of joy; at your right hand are pleasures forevermore. PSALM 16:11 ESV

REST FOR YOUR SOUL

"Come to Me, all you who are weary and burdened, and I will give you rest. Take My yoke upon you and learn from Me, for I am gentle and humble in heart, and you will find rest for your souls. For My yoke is easy and My burden is light." MATTHEW 11:28–30 NIV

Dear stroller, how are you doing so far? Are you enjoying keeping in step with Mary, Martha, and Jesus? So far, we started our walk with Mary and Martha in their hometown of Bethany, gleaning spiritual truths from their stories. Even though we have only just begun, today is a good day to pause in His presence and receive rest in the deepest part of our being, our souls.

We've all felt emotionally drained from time to time, haven't we? We think, *If I can just make it to the weekend, I'm going to catch up on my sleep.* Or, *If my child would only sleep in his/her own bed, I wouldn't be so tired all the time.* Or, *if I just had the means to hire someone to take care of my elderly parent, I could create space for myself.*

Life is busy. We oftentimes move at a pace that lends very little time to rest. But what if the most productive thing we could do for ourselves is slow down a bit and spend time with Jesus? How exactly can this be achieved? Well, the answer may not be as elusive as one may think.

Jesus knew we would experience intense weariness in our lives—circumstances beyond our control that leave us feeling depleted—yet we could come to Him for rest. Jesus humbled Himself to become a human being. Therefore, He knows exactly what it feels like to be tired. He also experienced sleepless nights and worrisome predicaments. How amazing to have a Savior who can relate to us in our times of worry and stress!

However, He beckons us to *"come to Him"* so He can give us rest for our souls. He can't take the burdens from us if we don't first enter into a deep and intimate relationship with God through Jesus Christ—one that involves surrendering our own will and concerns to Him. The life that Jesus offers us is easy and light. It's not our job to take on the responsibility of making sure that every circumstance works out. When we take Jesus at His word and allow those burdens to roll off of us and onto Him, we can find the rest we are so desperately needing.

When rest in Jesus, we learn what it means to be gentle and humble in heart. It's then that striving can cease and we are slower to judge and quicker to apologize. As we are diligent to come to Him, we find what we desire was there all along—rest for our souls.

- QUESTIONS -

It's reassuring to know that while Jesus walked on this earth He, too, experienced tiredness and depletion. How does this encourage you to come to Him to find your rest? How is His rest different from the rest the world offers you? How can you be more like Him in the ways of humbleness and gentleness?

To roll your burdens onto Jesus is like how a camel kneels to release the load it is carrying. Jesus wants you to roll off the heavy load you have been carrying onto Him because He can handle it. But you have to first come to Him. Are you experiencing a circumstance beyond your control that is keeping you up at night? Write to Him below and ask Him to take the burden from you.

_____

_____

_____

_____

_____

_____

_____

_____

Take a moment to reflect on what is most appealing about finding rest in Jesus. Describe what it would feel like to receive a soul rest. Record your thoughts here.

_____

_____

_____

_____

_____

_____

_____

_____

_____

SCRIPTURE

*Now that we know what we have—
Jesus, this great High Priest with
ready access to God—let's not let
it slip through our fingers. We don't
have a priest who is out of touch
with our reality. He's been through
weakness and testing, experienced
it all—all but the sin. So let's walk right
up to Him and get what He is
so ready to give. Take the mercy,
accept the help.*

HEBREWS 4:14–16 THE MESSAGE

*Rejoice in the Lord always. I will say
it again: Rejoice! Let your gentleness
be evident to all. The Lord is near.*

PHILIPPIANS 4:4–5 NIV

*Depend on the LORD;
trust Him, and He will
take care of you.*

PSALM 37:5 NCV

*Truly my soul finds rest in God;
my salvation comes from Him.
Yes, my soul, find rest in God;
my hope comes from Him.*

PSALM 62:1,5 NIV

PRAYER

Jesus, thank You for being a God who humbled Himself to this world. You didn't have to, but You did so that You would know exactly how I feel when I get tired, hot, thirsty, and lonely. You even know what it feels like to be stressed to the point of exhaustion. So I come to You now to ask that You revive my weary soul. Lord, I confess that I've been carrying around some things that are weighing me down. Will You please help me release these to You and, equally important, help me not pick them up again? Teach me how I can take my circumstances and know You've got me covered.

Instruct me on what it means to be humble and gentle like You. I'm sorry for all the times that the moment got too big for me and I was the opposite of humble and gentle. I allowed my arrogance and brashness to take over, even though I knew better. What a blessing it is to roll all that onto You now and know that I can start over with a clean slate. So again, I say "thank You" as I come to rest in You. Amen.

Moment to Breathe

Take a moment to breathe in God's rest and exhale out all your weariness. Imagine yourself walking through the desert land with what feels like a hundred pounds on your shoulders, when finally you come upon a refreshing stream. Jesus is there by the stream, and He reaches out His hand, inviting you to come to Him. He says He knows that you feel weary and heavy-laden. Oh, how relieving it is to know that He sees your tiredness and He understands it because He has been there too. As you dip your toes into the stream, He tells you to roll the things that are keeping you up at night onto Him because He can handle them. He has already gone before you, and you can simply rest because it is His responsibility to carry it, not yours. You want to cry from the relief of it all and wonder why you waited so long to come to Him. As you put your feet back on the dry ground, you find that you feel one hundred pounds lighter, because with Jesus the burdens are lifted. Take one final deep breath in and receive rest for your soul.

When the cares of my heart are many, your consolations cheer my soul.
PSALM 94:19 ESV

DON'T LET COMPARISON STEAL YOUR JOY

But Martha was distracted by her many tasks, and she came up and asked, "Lord, don't You care that my sister has left me to serve alone? So tell her to give me a hand." LUKE 10:40 CSB

President Theodore Roosevelt said, "Comparison is the thief of joy." When we compare our lives to others, we get robbed of the joy that is right before us. We think our summer vacation was amazing until we get on social media and see a friend's trip. We feel beautiful in a new dress until we see the same dress on another woman who just so happens to be a size or two different. What happened to all those warm and fuzzy feelings that were there a moment ago? They vanished like cotton candy does on our tongue, leaving us with sticky fingers as the lone reminder of how sweet our situation once was.

When Martha approached Jesus, we are told she "came up" to Him, implying that she stood next to Jesus before she asked Him her accusatory question. Now remember with me where Mary was during this time—she was contentedly sitting at Jesus's feet. Instead of gently sliding down next to Mary and receiving the rest she was desiring, Martha stood over her while pointedly asking Jesus if He even cared that Mary had so audaciously left her to serve alone. Martha was allowing her comparison to rob her of the joy that was right before her.

And here comes the million-dollar question: *"Lord, don't You care?"*

Lord, don't You care that I have served

You faithfully at my church, yet I've never been given any recognition?

Lord, don't You care that I stretch every penny while other families don't even give to the offering fund?

Lord, don't You care that I poured my heart and soul into that women's event, and no one even said thank you?

These are understandable questions. However, this question of "Lord, don't You care?" reveals much more about the state of our own hearts than the heart of God. Sometimes we feel like we are the only ones out there serving Him, and therefore we are due preferential treatment. But the truth is that when we come to Jesus with a spirit of comparison, it's difficult for us to receive all that He is ready to provide. In that frame of mind, it's difficult to obtain the thing we wanted in the first place—rest.

The antidote to comparison is contentment. When we learn how to stop asking questions like "Don't You care?" and replace them with a declaration of gratitude for what we have in front of us, we will stand a little taller and hold on to the joy we originally possessed. That's what happens when we rest in Jesus and trust Him to work out things on our behalf. And we typically find that's exactly what we wanted all along.

Reflection
- QUESTIONS -

Martha was looking at her situation through the lens of comparison when she should have focused more on contentment. Are there any situations in your life right now in which you have let the spirit of comparison rob you of your joy? Write them below, along with a list of ways you resist the temptation to compare your life to others.

Write out the words, Lord, don't You care? *and then put a big X over them. Then list two things for which you are grateful today.*

_____

_____

_____

_____

_____

_____

_____

_____

_____

What are some areas of your heart that need attention (i.e., unforgiveness or resentment)? What are some words that describe how you would feel if you were able to completely release these areas to God, allowing Him to give you complete rest?

_____

_____

_____

_____

_____

_____

_____

S C R I P T U R E

I am not saying this because I am in need, for I have learned to be content whatever the circumstances. I know what it is to be in need, and I know what it is to have plenty. I have learned the secret of being content in any and every situation, whether well fed or hungry, whether living in plenty or in want.

PHILIPPIANS 4:11–12 NIV

Pay careful attention to your own work, for then you will get the satisfaction of a job well done, and you won't need to compare yourself to anyone else.

GALATIANS 6:4 NLT

Therefore, as the chosen of God, holy and dearly loved, put on affection, compassion, kindness, humility, gentleness, patience, putting up with one another and forgiving one another. If anyone should have a complaint against anyone, just as also the Lord forgave you, thus also you do the same. And to all these things add love, which is the bond of perfection. And the peace of Christ must rule in your hearts, to which also you were called in one body, and be thankful.

COLOSSIANS 3:12–15 LEB

P R A Y E R

Jesus, I am sorry when I allow the spirit of comparison to bubble up inside of me. I know it is stealing my joy, and I ask that You help me to stop playing that game altogether. Instead of seeing what I am lacking, help me to see all the blessings I do have in front of me. And then help me to take it one step further and really be grateful for what You have given to me.

When I am tempted to let the question, "Lord, don't You care?" come out of my mouth, stop me in my tracks and show me how I can better rephrase the question or let go of it altogether. I do trust You to work things out on my behalf—please forgive me when I act like I don't. Show me if there are any areas of my heart that need to be tended to, and then let me be brave enough to address them head-on. Make me aware of opportunities to sit at Your feet, knowing You love me and You will work things out for my good. I love You, Jesus. Forgive me when I fall short. Amen.

Moment to Breathe

Take a moment to breathe in God's rest and exhale out your spirit of comparison. Imagine that you are at the state fair and everyone around you seems to be in high spirits. You can hear the squeals of delight from those on the rides and the excitement from those playing the booth games. You peacefully walk around the fair with the stuffed bear that you won and your cotton candy on a stick. But as you look around, you start to notice that other people are carrying bigger bears than yours and their cotton candy looks fluffier. Suddenly you are not enjoying your time at the fair and you wish you'd never come. But then Jesus is there, and He asks if you'd like to ride the Ferris wheel with Him. You unenthusiastically agree, but as you are lifted high into the night sky, you begin to see things differently. Everyone's bears and cotton candy seem small from up here, and you realize it was silly to let such comparisons steal your joy. You tell Jesus that you are grateful to be with Him in this moment and that you will remember how resting with Him is so much better than those toxic feelings. So take a deep breath in and receive back your joy.

When I am filled with cares, Your comfort brings me joy. PSALM 94:19 CSB

BETTER TOGETHER

But Martha was distracted by all the preparations that had to be made. She came to Him and asked, "Lord, don't You care that my sister has left me to do the work by myself? Tell her to help me!" LUKE 10:40 NIV

If you have ever been responsible for the success of a particular event or ministry, then you can appreciate the time and preparation it takes to pull it off. Having the right people helping in the right spaces is vital to success, and the bonus is that it allows both ourselves and others to use our various gifts. Those see the beauty in that reality often go on to create outstanding things, whereas those who go at it alone just end up exhausted.

With that in mind, let's step back into Martha's reality. How many onions had she diced while humming to herself? How much effort went into tenderizing the meat before she realized her arm was beginning to get sore? How many times had the broth nearly boiled over in the pot because she couldn't get there fast enough to stir it? There was an endless number of tasks to be done, and it seemed as if she was a one-woman show. It's no wonder Martha eventually found herself boiling over about being left alone in the kitchen with no help from Mary. After asking Jesus if He even cared about her circumstance, she finally blurted out, "Tell her to help me!" That exclamation point tells us everything we need to know about Martha's frame of mind—and then some.

But we as women understand that Martha's frustration wasn't unwarranted, be-cause it does take preparation to pull off such a feat. So the question becomes, how can we rest in Jesus when there is still work to be done? Perhaps it's as easy as reordering our to-do list.

The first action item would be to prioritize our time with God before launching into any work. Reading one chapter of the Bible and praying for a few minutes sets us on the most productive path possible. Next, we can consider asking the Lord to bring to mind anyone who may be gifted in the areas of help that we are needing. After making a phone call to set up a coffee date with that woman, we are able to share our vision with her to identify if her contribution would lend to its success. Then, we can watch in amazement as God works out the details.

When we are diligent to spend time with Jesus first, then we are filled and can serve His people better than if we resolve to do things in our own strength. Furthermore, when we invoke the help of our sister in a loving and respectful way, she gets to use her strengths to serve, which are undoubtably different than our own. It's then that the flower arrangements look more beautiful or the meal tastes more delicious or the ministry is more vibrant than if we had done it alone. The reality is that we are better together.

Reflection
- QUESTIONS -

Have you ever overseen the success of an event or ministry? Reflect on what worked and what you could do to make it better next time. What are some ways you can be "better together" with other women?

What gifts did God give you? What can you do to develop these gifts further?

_____

_____

_____

_____

_____

_____

_____

_____

_____

_____

Do you ever find yourself in Martha's shoes, short-tempered and exhausted from serving? Write a note to release that into Jesus's hands and ask Him in a respectful way to bring you the help you need.

_____

_____

_____

_____

_____

_____

_____

_____

SCRIPTURE

Don't think you are better than you really are. Be honest in your evaluation of yourselves, measuring yourselves by the faith God has given us. Just as our bodies have many parts and each part has a special function, so it is with Christ's body. We are many parts of one body, and we all belong to each other.

ROMANS 12:3–5 NLT

O how I love and treasure Your law; throughout the day I fill my heart with its light!

PSALM 119:97 TPT

All the believers were together and had everything in common. They sold property and possessions to give to anyone who had need. Every day they continued to meet together in the temple courts. They broke bread in their homes and ate together with glad and sincere hearts, praising God and enjoying the favor of all the people. And the Lord added to their number daily those who were being saved.

ACTS 2:44–47 NIV

PRAYER

Dear Lord, thank You for this lesson that we are better together when we work toward a goal for Your kingdom. I have seen myself in Martha and have felt her frustration and exhaustion when I try to do things without turning to You. I repent for the times when I have been short-tempered with my responses to others and even You.

Reveal and develop in me the spiritual gifts You have given to me. Give me opportunities to use them for Your glory. Thank You for a good body of believers whom I can use my gifts in tandem with. Don't let me be shy about my gifts, but give me a spirit of boldness, knowing I am working together with others for a common goal that will bring You honor.

Jesus, help me to be diligent to spend time with You before I begin my work each day, whether it be planning for something big or just an ordinary day. I know this is how I can rest better in You, so I commit to being "better together" with You first. I love You. Amen.

Moment to Breathe

Take a moment to breathe in God's rest and exhale out your frustration. Imagine you are at a banquet hall that has been beautifully decorated. You admire the sprays of white roses, the fabric of the seat backs, and a charcuterie board that is filled with delectables. As you fill your plate from the many different chafing dishes, you realize that no one person could have pulled off this magnificent of a reception. After eating, you make your way to the table where the cake stands. There you encounter Jesus, and He asks if you have met the woman serving the cake. You realize that you do know her and could actually use her help with your upcoming event. He graciously introduces you to a few more people, and by the time you leave you find that the weight of your responsibilities is lifted, and you feel peaceful and energized at the same time. After spending time with Jesus, you are filled with exactly what you need to get your work done. Take one more deep breath in and receive your focus for today.

Let every detail in your lives—words, actions, whatever—be done in the name of the Master, Jesus, thanking God the Father every step of the way.
COLOSSIANS 3:17 THE MESSAGE

LORD OF YOUR LIFE

And she had a sister called Mary, who sat at the Lord's feet and listened to his teaching. But Martha was distracted with much serving. And she went up to him and said, "Lord, do you not care that my sister has left me to serve alone? Tell her then to help me." LUKE 10:39–40 ESV

God. Yahweh. Father. Jesus. Lord. Savior. There are many different names for the Lord, and each one carries with it different meanings for our one great God. It's remarkable that we have a God who can be called upon by name and wants us to discover Him in new and fresh ways.

Each and every time that Mary and Martha addressed Jesus, they called Him "Lord." Why this term and not simply "Jesus"? It's because they were heralding Him as something special, something sacred. "Lord" is *Kyrios* in the Greek language, and it means "supernatural master over all."[4] Jesus was not only Mary and Martha's friend and dinner guest, but He was also their Master. This is why when He entered the room, Mary wanted to sit and listen to Him, and Martha wanted to please Him with her hospitality. Because when the supernatural Master of all things is present, things shift on earth and in the heavenlies.

When we accept Jesus's free gift of salvation, when we simply confess our sin and believe in Him, He becomes our Savior. However, as we continue to walk with Him, He becomes not only our Savior, but also the Lord of our lives. When we call Him by this name of "Lord," we are giving Him access as Master of our lives. He no longer is relegated to the God we worship on Sunday, but He becomes much more personal than that. He is Master over our relationships, our jobs, our finances, our possessions, our health, our very being. He is Lord over all.

When Jesus entered the home of Mary and Martha, they didn't refuse Him the right to go into the back part of their home by saying, "Oh, I'm so sorry, Lord, but You are only allowed in the living room. That closet in the back is off-limits." No, as Master, He was allowed into every space of their home.

Jesus wants to be Master of every part of our lives. And as we learn to rest in Jesus, what we learn is that it's actually freeing to submit to Him as our Master, because that means He is in control, and we don't have to hold it all together. He is the One who created this amazing earth, and He alone keeps it spinning on its axis. If He is the supernatural Master over science, how much more should He be over our lives?

As we walk out this faith journey with Jesus, seeking rest from Him, the best thing we can do is swing wide every door of our being and make Him not just the Savior of our souls, but also the Lord of our lives.

---

[4] James Swanson, *Dictionary of Biblical Languages with Semantic Domains: Greek (New Testament)* (Oak Harbor: Logos Research Systems, Inc., 1997), "kyrios."

Reflection
- QUESTIONS -

Describe what you think it might feel like to have Jesus enter your house, to be in the presence of the "supernatural Master over all"?

_____

_____

_____

_____

_____

_____

_____

_____

_____

_____

_____

_____

_____

_____

_____

_____

_____

_____

_____

_____

Have you ever thought about Jesus being your Savior versus being your Lord? How do you personally view the difference between the two? How can you worship Him today as both Savior and Lord of your life?

_____

_____

_____

_____

_____

_____

_____

_____

_____

List some areas of your life that you want to see Jesus come into as your Lord. Give Him permission to infiltrate every space.

_____

_____

_____

_____

_____

_____

_____

_____

_____

SCRIPTURE

"Be dressed, ready for service, and have your lamps shining. Be like servants who are waiting for their master to come home from a wedding party. When he comes and knocks, the servants immediately open the door for him. They will be blessed when their master comes home, because he sees that they were watching for him. I tell you the truth, the master will dress himself to serve and tell the servants to sit at the table, and he will serve them. Those servants will be blessed when he comes in and finds them still waiting, even if it is midnight or later."

LUKE 12:35–38 NCV

The way I love you is like the way a servant wants to please his master, the way a maid waits for the orders of her mistress. We look to You, our God, with passionate longing to please You and discover more of Your mercy and grace.

PSALM 123:2 TPT

In the presence of God, who gives life to all, and of Christ Jesus, who gave a good confession before Pontius Pilate, I charge you to keep this command without fault or failure until the appearing of our Lord Jesus Christ. God will bring this about in His own time. He is the blessed and only Sovereign, the King of kings, and the Lord of lords, who alone is immortal and who lives in unapproachable light, whom no one has seen or can see, to Him be honor and eternal power. Amen.

I TIMOTHY 6:13–16 CSB

PRAYER

Jesus, I worship You today as not only my Savior, but also the Lord of my life. Thank You for dying for me, for laying down Your life for mine. You didn't hold anything back from me, so today I resolve not to hold anything back from You. I give You permission to infiltrate every space of my life—my relationships, job, finances. . .even my innermost thoughts. I want You to be present in everything because with You are light and life. Illuminate the areas in which I have been resisting Your presence, and let me be brave enough to trust You in these places. I know it is not my job to hold the whole world together. That responsibility belongs to You. So teach me how to let go and let You be the supernatural Master over it all. As I journey along with Mary and Martha, learning to rest in You, show me how to enjoy You as they did. I don't want You to be relegated to a God I only worship on Sunday, but I want You to be Master every day of the week. Teach me how to let You in as my Lord to stay! In the Lord Jesus's name. Amen.

Moment to Breathe

Take a moment to breathe in God's rest and exhale out your reservations. Imagine that you are outside watering your plants when Jesus walks up and asks if He can come inside. You immediately put away the garden hose and invite Him in without hesitation. You are grateful to have Him at your home because you know that without Him, you would not have forgiveness for your sins and you would be destined for a terrible life. But because of His sacrifice, your sins are forgiven and you are secured to have eternal life with Him. As He starts to move freely throughout your home, though, you find you are a little nervous for Him to step into the other rooms. Why? If He is your Master, then He is responsible for every room. So you begin to let go of controlling what lies behind the other doors and you allow Him access. As you do, feel yourself resting in His sovereignty and His ability to hold it all together. With that in mind, take a deep breath in and receive your release into His Lordship.

When they heard this, they raised their voices together to God and said, "Master, You are the one who made the heaven, the earth, and the sea, and everything in them."
ACTS 4:24 CSB

HE CALLS YOU
BY NAME

But the Lord answered and said to her, "Martha, Martha, you are worried and bothered about so many things." LUKE 10:41 NASB1995

Do you ever find yourself struggling to remember people's names when they first introduce themselves? Typically at a first introduction, we are so hyper-focused on what we are going to say that we oftentimes completely miss the name that comes out of the other person's mouth. *Oh, no. Did she say Amy or Amanda*? Such encounters can lead to some quite embarrassing future conversations.

Yet it is wonderfully reassuring to know that Jesus never forgets a name, and even more astounding is the fact that He knew us before the foundations of the world were even created! As we've discovered, the Lord allows us to know Him by different names, but He also calls us by name. He is a relational God, and He knows us because He formed us, but He also delights when we make an effort to get to know Him.

When Martha came to Jesus with her complaint, Jesus didn't look at her and say, *"Now, who are you again?"* Rather, Scripture says that He took the time to answer her, and before He did, He called her by name. And not just once, but twice.

Actually, by having her name spoken twice, Martha is placed in good company. Abraham, Jacob, Moses, Samuel, Simon, and Saul (aka Paul) are all called by name twice by the Almighty, each with an invi-

tation to move into a new space with Him. Abraham was invited into sacrifice and faith (Genesis 22:1–19). Jacob was told not to fear as he traveled to Egypt to find his long-lost son, Joseph (Genesis 46:1–4). Moses and Samuel were invited into their calling (Exodus 3:1–12; I Samuel 3:1–10). Simon was invited into a faith that would not fail and a call to strengthen his brothers once he turned back after his sifting (Luke 22:31–32; John 21:15–17). And Saul received an invitation to forsake the life he knew and transform into Paul, who was to be a witness to all people that Jesus was indeed the Messiah (Acts 9:1–19).

Here, as Jesus gently calls Martha's name twice, He is inviting her to a space of rest—and He invites us to the same space.

It may be that we are too busy to hear when He quietly whispers our name, so a quick double take is necessary to get our attention. He isn't being unkind in His call of our name, or even perturbed. Instead, He is being the caring God that He is, relational at His core, intimately knowing us and our tendencies to wander. In the double call of our names, He is inviting us to know Him and His heart better. Like Martha, we are redirected to slow down and hear His voice as He beckons us to come and rest in Him.

Reflection
- QUESTIONS -

Write about a time when you knew God was trying to get your attention. How did He go about doing it?

_____

_____

_____

_____

_____

_____

_____

_____

_____

_____

_____

_____

_____

_____

_____

_____

_____

_____

_____

_____

What is your view of God as it pertains to His desire to have a relationship with you? Name some ways you can deepen your relationship with Him today.

_____

_____

_____

_____

_____

_____

_____

_____

_____

Close your eyes and picture the Lord calling your name twice. Into what new space do you feel He wants to invite you to enter? Record what is revealed to you below.

_____

_____

_____

_____

_____

_____

_____

_____

SCRIPTURE

Long before He laid down earth's foundations, He had us in mind, had settled on us as the focus of His love, to be made whole and holy by His love.

EPHESIANS 1:3–4 THE MESSAGE

"The one who enters by the door is the shepherd of the sheep. The one who guards the door opens it for him. And the sheep listen to the voice of the shepherd. He calls his own sheep by name and leads them out."

JOHN 10:2–3 NCV

About noon as I came near Damascus, suddenly a bright light from heaven flashed around me. I fell to the ground and heard a voice say to me, "Saul! Saul! Why do you persecute Me?"
"Who are You, Lord?" I asked.
"I am Jesus of Nazareth, whom you are persecuting," He replied. My companions saw the light, but they did not understand the voice of Him who was speaking to me.
"What shall I do, Lord?" I asked.
"Get up," the Lord said, "and go into Damascus. There you will be told all that you have been assigned to do." My companions led me by the hand into Damascus, because the brilliance of the light had blinded me. A man named Ananias came to see me. He was a devout observer of the law and highly respected by all the Jews living there. He stood beside me and said, "Brother Saul, receive your sight!" And at that very moment I was able to see him.

ACTS 22:6–13 NIV

PRAYER

Jesus, what an amazing, relational God You are! You know my name, and You call it over and over again, inviting me into a space of rest in You. Forgive me when I tuned You out, not accepting Your invitation to be in a relationship with You. Forgive me when I heard You calling my name but I let myself be distracted from coming to rest in You. Forgive me when I heard You say my name twice but I thought Your heart was not for me and that You were being unkind.

Deepen my faith like Abraham's, confirm my calling like Samuel's, and bring me back to You time and again like Simon. Give me a chance to refocus and rest like You did for Martha. Let me be like Paul and use my life to witness to others.

I praise You today for Your sweet redirection, for the tender way You speak to me, for caring enough to call me by name. In return, let Your name ever be on my lips. Amen.

Moment to Breathe

Take a moment to breathe in God's rest and exhale out any false notions of Him being an unrelational God. Imagine yourself at the back of a tour bus while on a much-anticipated trip to the Holy Land. Jesus is your tour guide, and He is pointing out the various sites as the bus makes its way up to Nazareth. He is telling a story of how He played as a boy in this very same Jezreel Valley, but as He continues to talk, you find that you are distracted by what could be going on at home. *Did you pay your energy bill? Are the caretakers caring for your pet properly?* You snap out of it when you hear your name being called twice over the PA system. At first your face turns red with embarrassment until you realize that Jesus was not being unkind and He isn't even perturbed with you. He simply didn't want you to miss the moment right in front of you. You turn your attention back to Him and become enraptured by His childhood stories, knowing that it gives you a better understanding of who He is at the core—a kind, relational God. Take another deep breath in and receive His calling into your new space.

"Before I shaped you in the womb, I knew all about you. Before you saw the light of day, I had holy plans for you." JEREMIAH 1:5 THE MESSAGE

A HOLY REST

By the seventh day God had finished the work He had been doing; so on the seventh day He rested from all His work. Then God blessed the seventh day and made it holy, because on it He rested from all the work of creating that He had done. GENESIS 2:2–3 NIV

It's been said that those who contribute to society, or work, tend to be happier and more satisfied in their lives. Of course, we all can agree that work can provide large degrees of stress as well, but generally speaking, work is a good thing for us as humans.

God used this same concept at the beginning of creation. After each day of creating the world and everything in it, God would examine it and deem it to be "good." His work was so good, in fact, that it is still astounding the best of astronomers, anthropologists, and philosophers to this very day. But what is equally amazing is that our God, who is capable of creating all that science has to offer, decided it was important to rest after doing so. He set aside a full day, what we know of as the Sabbath, and *"made it holy, because on it He rested from all the work of creating that He had done."*

God also carved out this time of Sabbath rest for the Israelites, as a part of His lasting covenant to them. It was a gift to His chosen people, who had been enslaved by the Egyptians. He gave them a day to cease their activity and rest, just as He had done for Himself at creation. It was a day to be celebrated (Deuteronomy 5:12–15).

God Himself didn't need to rest after the creation of the world, but He did it to show mankind the beauty of ceasing activity within a designated time for the purpose of rest and refreshment. He knew that times of refreshing come when we take the time to rest our minds and bodies. Without these parameters and if left to our own devices, we are in danger of letting our work move from being beneficial to hazardous for our health.

However, the biggest reason God wants us to rest from our work is so we can spend time with Him. Sabbath is a chance to pause in His presence and quiet our hearts and minds. It ushers in the anticipation of being rewarded for a week's worth of hard work as well as a time to refocus in anticipation of what He may have in store for the next week. It is a celebration of our freedom as we worship the One who has set us free. It was made to meet our needs, knowing that He is Lord over it all.

There most certainly is a time to work, but there is also a time to rest—a chance to refresh our minds and bodies so that we can be the best versions of ourselves.

Reflection
- QUESTIONS -

Describe a time when you took a moment (or a day) to refresh your mind.

Is there a particular day of the week that you set aside to rest from your work so that you can pause in His presence and worship Him? Describe what that looks like or what you desire it to look like.

_____

_____

_____

_____

_____

_____

_____

_____

Has there ever been a time when you felt like Martha and worked yourself into a state of exhaustion? Reflecting on that time, what can you do differently next time you find yourself in a similar scenario?

_____

_____

_____

_____

_____

_____

_____

_____

SCRIPTURE

Then Jesus said to them, "The Sabbath was made to meet the needs of people, and not people to meet the requirements of the Sabbath. So the Son of Man is Lord, even over the Sabbath!"

MARK 2:27–28 NLT

There remains, then, a Sabbath-rest for the people of God; for anyone who enters God's rest also rests from their works, just as God did from His.

HEBREWS 4:9–10 NIV

Then the LORD said to Moses, "Say to the Israelites, 'You must observe My Sabbaths. This will be a sign between Me and you for the generations to come, so you may know that I am the LORD, who makes you holy.
" 'Observe the Sabbath, because it is holy to you. Anyone who desecrates it is to be put to death; those who do any work on that day must be cut off from their people. For six days work is to be done, but the seventh day is a day of sabbath rest, holy to the LORD. Whoever does any work on the Sabbath day is to be put to death. The Israelites are to observe the Sabbath, celebrating it for the generations to come as a lasting covenant. It will be a sign between Me and the Israelites forever, for in six days the LORD made the heavens and the earth, and on the seventh day He rested and was refreshed.' "

EXODUS 31:12–17 NIV

P R A Y E R

Lord, first I want to take a minute to exclaim how awesome You are to have created this beautiful world. It's beyond my comprehension, but with each day that I wake up again to behold Your masterpiece, I marvel at what a creative and powerful God You are. It's also a marvelous discovery to know that You as God chose to rest after the creation of the world. You did so that I could know that rest is good and beneficial—if it was necessary for You, then it's necessary for me. Thank You for the gift of work. I understand and value

the concept of a job well done, and I aim to do it to Your glory. Forgive me for the times when I have been lazy at my job, and help me to do better next time. Forgive me also for not prioritizing a time to rest and working myself into a state of exhaustion. Let me look to You as my resting place, and let me find satisfaction in taking a holy rest week in and week out. Create the desire within me to eat with family, read Your Word, and worship You with other believers. I look to You for the rest I so desperately need. Amen.

Moment to Breathe

Take a moment to breathe in God's rest and exhale out your exhaustion. Imagine you are outside on a cloudless night. The sun has just gone down, and as the moon and stars start to make their way into the night sky, you feel the drain of your workweek begin to melt away. As you allow your heart and mind to quiet, your thoughts begin to shift to this great God of yours who created this night for you. As the stars begin to twinkle, you think of how faithful He has been in your life, and it hits you all over again that the God who holds the universe together, holds you in this moment as well. He has never let you down, and He won't start now. As the cool night breeze blows, you allow yourself to pause in His presence and worship Him as your Creator and Sustainer. You feel Him reaffirm that He sees how hard you are working, yet He also knows you need to regularly cease activity so you can be the best version of yourself again next week. So you pause for a moment longer and refocus your mind. Take one final deep breath in and receive His holy rest.

One hand full of rest is better than two fists full of labor and striving after wind.
ECCLESIASTES 4:6 NASB1995

GOD HIMSELF

DIDN'T *NEED* TO REST

AFTER THE CREATION

OF THE WORLD,

BUT HE DID IT

TO SHOW MANKIND

THE BEAUTY OF CEASING ACTIVITY

WITHIN A DESIGNATED TIME

FOR THE PURPOSE OF

REST AND

REFRESHMENT.

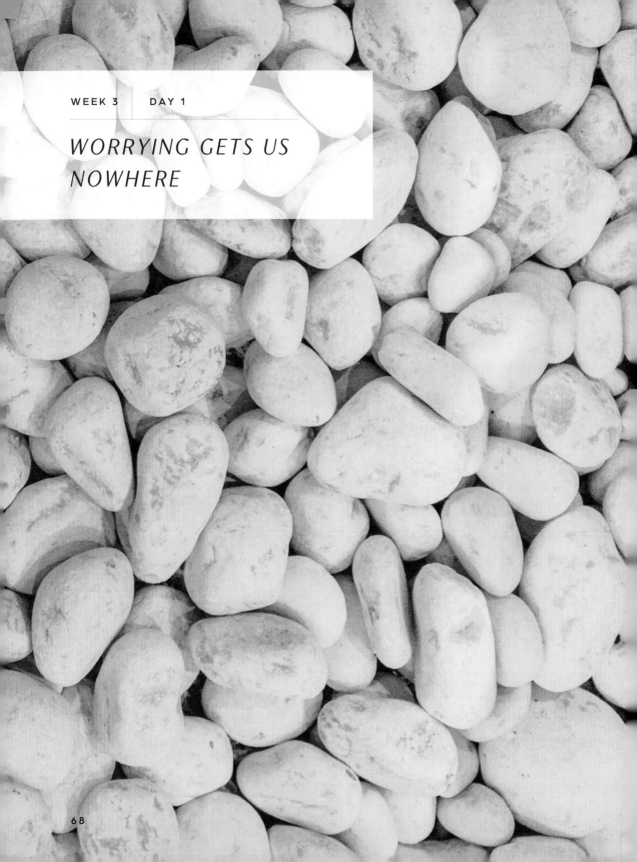

WORRYING GETS US NOWHERE

But the Lord answered and said to her, "Martha, Martha, you are worried and bothered about so many things." LUKE 10:41 NASB1995

One of the remarkable things about Scripture is that it spans the scope of human feelings and emotions. There are psalms on both heartache and rejoicing (Psalm 13). The book of Acts records a sharp disagreement that broke out between two great ministers of the Gospel (Acts 15:36-41). In Song of Songs, we find chapters on romantic love (Song of Songs 1:2-4). And among the pages of the Bible there are clear instructions on how to battle fear and anxiety (Philippians 4:6-7; I Peter 5:7; Isaiah 41:10; Psalm 56:3; Psalm 34:4; Matthew 6:25-27; Psalm 23:4; II Timothy 1:7; Joshua 1:9; Psalm 94:19, to name a few).

Anxiety is one of those things that can creep up on us. At first we may have a small concern, which turns into a worry, but before long we are panicked over what "could happen," letting anxiety take root in us. According to the Office on Women's Health, women are twice as likely as men to be diagnosed with an anxiety disorder, which can lead to serious physical health issues. Anxiety can rob us of sleep, productivity, and even our appetites, leaving us with a poor quality of life.

Perhaps this is why Jesus sought to hit anxiety head-on with His teachings. He said that we are not to worry about our lives, not even the details of what we will eat, what we will drink, or the clothing we wear. For if our heavenly Father takes care of the birds, how much more will He take care of our needs? At its root, worry robs us of trusting the Lord to meet our needs. We falsely believe that if we worry, we can invoke some kind of control over our situation, but in reality, God is the One who is in control and has the power to change our situations.

Jesus knew this as He gently pointed out to Martha that she was worried and bothered about so many inconsequential things. She came to Jesus with feelings of injustice, but He saw right through her to the root of the problem—she wasn't trusting Him to provide her every need. Instead of receiving affirmation for her perceived injustice, Jesus looked deep into her soul and spoke directly to the problem, just as He does time and again for us as well.

There are serious circumstances we will face in life that cannot be ignored. It's part of living in a fallen world. But when we worry about trivial things that may or may not happen, that's when we are in danger of wasting our lives away.

If God was intentional enough to care for the birds, how much more will He be faithful to care for you and me? He knows that worrying will get us nowhere and that the better option is to simply trust Him.

Reflection
- QUESTIONS -

Has worrying ever affected you or a loved one physically? How about spiritually? Write about how you got through it and what you learned from it.

_____

_____

_____

_____

_____

_____

_____

_____

_____

_____

_____

_____

_____

_____

_____

_____

_____

_____

_____

_____

_____

_____

_____

List out the things that are worrying and bothering you today. Let Him know that even though you don't see the end to the situation that's worrying you, you trust Him to take care of you.

What are some verses you can use to combat anxiety the next time it creeps up on you? Write them out here.

SCRIPTURE

"This is why I tell you to never be worried about your life, for all that you need will be provided, such as food, water, clothing—everything your body needs. Isn't there more to your life than a meal? Isn't your body more than clothing?

"Consider the birds—do you think they worry about their existence? They don't plant or reap or store up food, yet your heavenly Father provides them each with food. Aren't you much more valuable to your Father than they? So, which one of you by worrying could add anything to your life?

"And why would you worry about your clothing? Look at all the beautiful flowers of the field. They don't work or toil, and yet not even Solomon in all his splendor was robed in beauty more than one of these! So if God has clothed the meadow with hay, which is here for such a short time and then dried up and burned, won't He provide for you the clothes you need—you of little faith?

"So then, forsake your worries! Why would you say, 'What will we eat?' or 'What will we drink?' or 'What will we wear?' For that is what the unbelievers chase after. Doesn't your heavenly Father already know the things your bodies require?

"So above all, constantly seek God's kingdom and His righteousness, then all these less important things will be given to you abundantly."

MATTHEW 6:25–33 TPT

Do not be anxious about anything, but in every situation, by prayer and petition, with thanksgiving, present your requests to God. And the peace of God, which transcends all understanding, will guard your hearts and your minds in Christ Jesus.

PHILIPPIANS 4:6–7 NIV

P R A Y E R

Dear Jesus, I know that worrying gets me nowhere, so today I resolve to put my trust in You. Sometimes this life seems over-whelming, and there are so many things that need my attention. But if You have promised to take care of the birds, even to the point of dressing and feeding them, I know that You will take care of me. Teach me how to trust You like they do. Show me how to cast my anxiety upon You, knowing that You are able to handle it. Give me full confidence that I don't have to carry any of this weight I have put on myself, but that You will provide for me. Help me to release my perceived control. I resolve to come to You the next time I feel burdened and al-low You to take it from me, just as You were willing to do for Martha. I know that I am not alone. You are with me, and You fill me with Your perfect peace. Thank You for lov-ing me and caring for me like You do. I love You, too. Amen.

Moment to Breathe

Take a moment to breathe in God's rest and exhale out your worry. Collect all the things that have been bothering you into a knapsack or even a duffel bag if you need it. Then imagine yourself walking outside with your bag and meeting Jesus under the shade of a tree. You know He is willing to take the bag from you, but for whatever reason, you are not quite ready to part with it yet. As you sit down un-derneath the tree, you hear the birds chirping above. They are carefree and happy to sing their song. Jesus tells you that He cares for you even more than these birds. He reminds you that He can handle all the weight you have been carrying around. It's not your responsibility—it's His, and you can trust Him. He opens up His hands to receive your bag of worries, and you hand it over to Him. Instantly you feel lighter, freer than you have ever been. And even though the circumstances and needs are all still there, you are not carrying them, because Jesus is in control and you are free to sing like the birds. So take a deep breath in and receive your song.

Cast all your anxiety on Him because He cares for you. I PETER 5:7 NIV

THE BETTER CHOICE

"Only one thing is important. Mary has chosen the better thing, and it will never be taken away from her." LUKE 10:42 NCV

Some concepts in Scripture require a "both/and" mentality. For instance, Jesus was *both* fully human *and* fully God. God exhibits attributes of both justice and compassion. In Mary and Martha's example, both sitting and serving are necessary for the Christian life.

Yet, as we have seen, the timing of these two opposite actions is what matters to the heart of God. We can serve diligently, but if we neglect to spend time with Him, then it was all for naught. We can sit at His feet religiously, but if we don't ever put into practice all that we have learned, then we aren't being as effective for the Kingdom as we should be.

At the end of the day, one choice does outweigh the other, and that's exactly where Mary was content to be—as close as she could possibly be to Jesus. It's not that Jesus was slighting Martha and her hospitality. He was simply putting into perspective the truth that without spending time with Him, we may have offered our service, but we may not be doing it for the right reasons. Many philanthropists do wonderful things to help erase poverty. Many people serve faithfully in the soup kitchen week after week. But if Jesus is not part of the service, there is no hope!

The better choice is to consistently spend time with Jesus so that we can reflect His light and hope out into a dark and hurting world. At first we may not see the results, but as we sit at His feet day after day, we find that we begin to talk more like Him, think more like Him, walk more like Him, and act more like Him. And before we know it, other people are asking us about the light and hope we have even in the midst of hardship. It's then that we can take them by the hand and lead them to the feet of Jesus.

Mary and Martha have given us a glimpse of how two women with different dispositions can use their gifts to bless Jesus. They both welcomed Jesus into their hearts and home, and because they did, we are able to learn valuable lessons from them on how to rest in Jesus even when there is still work to be done, even when women were not esteemed at the same level as men in their day and age, and even when burdens seem heavy—because resting in Jesus has more to do with trusting that He is Lord over our challenges and circumstances than it does ceasing all activity.

The choice to rest in Jesus is ours to make. It won't come by happenstance because there will always be distractions. Yet choosing to be in His presence is always the right choice. And once we are there, we realize there is absolutely nothing better.

Reflection
- QUESTIONS -

It can be challenging to accept a "both/and" perspective when we are accustomed to giving a right or wrong answer. In what ways have you seen certain attributes of God as "both/and" in your life?

With which sister do you identify more and why? Why do you think Jesus said Mary had made the better choice when Jesus Himself was a servant?

_____

_____

_____

_____

_____

_____

_____

_____

_____

_____

Ask Jesus to help you consistently choose to rest in Him despite your challenges and circumstances. Offer your prayer to Him here.

_____

_____

_____

_____

_____

_____

_____

_____

_____

_____

SCRIPTURE

Adopt the same attitude
as that of Christ Jesus,
who, existing in the form of God,
did not consider equality with God
as something to be exploited.
Instead He emptied Himself
by assuming the form of a servant,
taking on the likeness of humanity.
And when He had come as a man,
He humbled Himself by
becoming obedient
to the point of death—
even to death on a cross.
For this reason God
highly exalted Him
and gave Him the name
that is above every name,
so that at the name of Jesus
every knee will bow—
in heaven and on earth
and under the earth—
and every tongue will confess
that Jesus Christ is Lord,
to the glory of God the Father.

PHILIPPIANS 2:5–11 CSB

So now wrap your hearts tightly
around the hope that lives within us,
knowing that God always keeps His
promises! Discover creative ways to
encourage others and to motivate
them toward acts of compassion,
doing beautiful works as
expressions of love.

HEBREWS 10:23–24 TPT

P R A Y E R

O Lord, what a sweet gift I have received in witnessing how You love and esteemed both Mary and Martha. I have learned so much from these two sisters already, and I can see a little bit of myself in both of them. I know that being a servant is important to You, yet being in Your presence on a consistent basis is more important. Redirect me when I get those priorities out of order. Help me to make the better choice each and every day. Also help me to include You in the way I serve others. I don't want to be just another woman doing kind things, I want to offer the world the hope and light that You provide! Jesus, also help me to remember the lessons I have learned so far about resting in You and how it has more to do with trusting Your heart than it does anything else. You are Lord over my challenges and circumstances, and I give them to You all over again today. Today I choose Your presence. Today I choose to rest. Today I choose You, Jesus! Amen.

Moment to Breathe

Take a moment to breathe in God's rest and exhale out your challenges. Imagine you have entered a dark room and you can hear the distressed cries of people around you. You don't know where the breaker is or how to get the electricity back on, but what you do have is a flashlight in your pocket. You take it out and offer its light to those around you. You are not the source of light, but because you possess it, you can guide others out of the darkness. They are grateful for your service, but you are careful not to keep the praise for yourself. You tell them about where you found your light and how they can get their own flashlight so they can help other people get out of the dark. Then, as you return home, you make sure to put your flashlight on the charger so it will work again tomorrow, because without spending time on that charger, the light will go dim. This is a choice that you make day after day even though there are various circumstances and challenges that try to get in your way. Yet you choose wisely so that your light can shine. Take one more deep breath in and receive His source of light.

Let the dawning day bring me revelation of Your tender, unfailing love. Give me light for my path and teach me, for I trust in You. PSALM 143:8 TPT

TO BE LOVED

Now a man named Lazarus was sick. He was from Bethany, the village of Mary and her sister Martha. (This Mary, whose brother Lazarus now lay sick, was the same one who poured perfume on the Lord and wiped His feet with her hair.) So the sisters sent word to Jesus, "Lord, the one You love is sick." JOHN 11:1–3 NIV

Now Jesus loved Martha and her sister and Lazarus. JOHN 11:5 NIV

It's time to walk a different path. A path that may seem dark at the onset, but it won't stay that way when the Light of the World shows up to walk beside us.

We've had the benefit of listening in on the conversation had between Jesus and Martha and were able to observe the varying personalities of the two sisters. We also witnessed Jesus's affection for them both as individuals. God's Word has given us a gift because now, as we walk once again with Mary and Martha, we can better understand their reactions when the unthinkable happens.

But before we get ahead of ourselves, let's take our first step into the story found in John 11. We learn from the get-go that the brother of Mary and Martha, named Lazarus, is sick. (John identifies Mary as the *"one who poured perfume on the Lord and wiped His feet with her hair,"* which is a story we will later discuss.) John records, *"So the sisters sent word to Jesus, 'Lord, the one You love is sick.'"* Notice that Mary and Martha didn't call Lazarus by name; they simply identified him as "the one You love." That description alone was enough for Jesus to recognize "the one" as Lazarus.

The Greek word used for "love" is *phileō*, which is a brotherly, affectionate love based on a close association with that person. It's the kind of love you and I have for our closest friends who walk beside us on a consistent basis. With each step taken, we develop a greater sense of loyalty and affection for her. This is how Mary and Martha describe Jesus's love for Lazarus.

But Jesus uses a different verb to describe the love He has for Lazarus, Mary, and Martha. Scripture says, *"Now Jesus loved Martha and her sister and Lazarus."* The Greek word for "love" used here is *agapaō*, which is a sacrificial love that is demonstrated or shown. This is the love that is described in Romans 5:8: God proved His love for us by having Jesus die on the cross for our sins. It's a love that is tested and proven to be true.

Jesus loved Lazarus and his sisters in both an affectionate and a sacrificial way, and He loves us like that too. But it is worth noting that the intimacy that comes with a *phileō* love is created by spending time together. It's only then that we can begin to understand the deep, demonstrated love of *agapaō*. Oftentimes, we limit God's love to our level, but His love runs deeper than we can ever imagine.

Reflection
- QUESTIONS -

Think of a few of your closest relationships—the people you have an affectionate love for. List their name(s) below. Now think of those you have felt a deep, sacrificial love for. List their name(s) below. Write out the difference in your own words.

Do you feel as if you have limited in the past, or are currently limiting, the depth of God's love for you? In what ways can you erase those limits?

_____

_____

_____

_____

_____

_____

_____

_____

_____

_____

Lazarus was not mentioned by name but rather as "the one You love" when word was sent to Jesus. Do you view yourself as "the one You love" by Jesus? Write down a few steps you need to take today to show Jesus that you trust His heart for you.

_____

_____

_____

_____

_____

_____

_____

_____

_____

SCRIPTURE

For when the time was right, the Anointed One came and died to demonstrate His love for sinners who were entirely helpless, weak, and powerless to save themselves. Now, would anyone dare to die for the sake of a wicked person? We can all understand if someone was willing to die for a truly noble person. But Christ proved God's passionate love for us by dying in our place while we were still lost and ungodly!

ROMANS 5:6–8 TPT

And I pray that you, being rooted and established in love, may have power, together with all the Lord's holy people, to grasp how wide and long and high and deep is the love of Christ, and to know this love that surpasses knowledge—that you may be filled to the measure of all the fullness of God.

EPHESIANS 3:17–19 NIV

My beloved friends, let us continue to love each other since love comes from God. Everyone who loves is born of God and experiences a relationship with God. The person who refuses to love doesn't know the first thing about God, because God is love—so you can't know Him if you don't love. This is how God showed His love for us: God sent His only Son into the world so we might live through Him. This is the kind of love we are talking about—not that we once upon a time loved God, but that He loved us and sent His Son as a sacrifice to clear away our sins and the damage they've done to our relationship with God. My dear, dear friends, if God loved us like this, we certainly ought to love each other. No one has seen God, ever. But if we love one another, God dwells deeply within us, and His love becomes complete in us— perfect love!

I JOHN 4:7–12 THE MESSAGE

PRAYER

Jesus, to be loved by You is both exhilarating and overwhelming at the same time. Sometimes I feel like I am not worthy of Your love or that I can never possibly love as deeply as You do, so why even try? But then I feel You calling me into a deeper relationship with You, and as I let myself be enveloped in Your love, I find that I can trust You more and more. Forgive me for when I limit my perception of Your love to what my small mind can comprehend. Help me to love You with a deep *agapeo* love and not just an affectionate *phileo* love. And when I fall short, as I am sure to do, give me grace and the desire to want to try again tomorrow. Thank You for always meeting me where I am, yet encouraging me to step out further with You.

I love You, Jesus. Amen.

Moment to Breathe

Take a moment to breathe in God's rest and exhale out your limitations. Imagine that you are on the field of an open-aired football stadium. When you look up to the sky, you can see the clouds moving, and you squint your eyes against the brightness of the sun. As you return your focus to the stands, you see the faces of those you love with a deep, proven love sitting in a small section. Then, with every blink you take, several more seats fill with people whom you feel loyal to—a close co-worker, a childhood friend, a special aunt or uncle. As you continue to blink, more and more faces of those you have affection for fill the stadium, but even with all those combined, the stadium is only a fraction of the way filled. Then Jesus joins you on the field. As He does, the stadium instantly fills to capacity, and you know, without even having to ask Him, that He loves every single one of them, plus countless others. With that in mind, take a deep breath in and receive your demonstrated love from Him.

For this is how God loved the world: He gave His one and only Son, so that everyone who believes in Him will not perish but have eternal life. JOHN 3:16 NLT

IT'S ALL ABOUT WHO GETS THE GLORY

"Lazarus's sickness will not end in death. No, it happened for the glory of God so that the Son of God will receive glory from this." JOHN 11:4 NLT

Have you ever struggled to know your purpose in life? It's important that we understand that our life matters, but that's not the same as our purpose. When we ponder our purpose, we ask questions like: *What are we really here for? Why is it necessary that we wake up to begin another day here on planet earth? What can I do to make my life count for something bigger than me?*

It's simple, really. Our chief purpose is to glorify God. Which means that we are to praise and honor God with the things we do and say so that we point others to Him. Jesus said during His Sermon on the Mount that we are to let our lights shine so when others see the good things we do, they will glorify our Father in heaven (see Matthew 5:16). If we are Christ followers, then none of our good works should be done with the hope of bringing ourselves glory. They should be done with the purpose of giving the Father the honor and praise He is due.

With that in mind, let's take another step into Martha and Mary's world. When we last visited them, they had sent word to Jesus that the one He loved was sick. Jesus responded rather cryptically to His disciples by stating that Lazarus's sickness woud not end in death. Whew! But wait, there's more. He said, *"No, it happened for the glory of God so that the Son of God will receive glory from this."* Hold up. What is *"this"* that You speak of, Jesus?

Jesus just gave the purpose of what is about to unfold before the disciples' eyes. *"It"* hadn't even happened yet, but Jesus wants the "why" behind it all to be clearly stated. It was so that God would be glorified and Jesus would receive the honor He is due as the Son of God.

Even Jesus, the Son of God, did His good works so the Father would get the glory and then so He as the Son would be glorified. Jesus was intentional in His actions, knowing they would eventually lead Him to be recognized as the Messiah. Lazarus's sickness had purpose, and that purpose would ultimately lead to God getting the glory.

As the disciples surely let out a sigh of temporary relief, so can we. It's not for us to hold the world together. That's His job. Ours is simply to be a light to the world and live in such a way that when people see the good things we do, they will want to give this great God of ours the praise He is due. What a great purpose to have in this life!

Reflection
- QUESTIONS -

The disciples were given the purpose of Lazarus's death before it even transpired, yet they weren't given the specifics. Have you ever experienced a time in your life when God reassured you that everything would be okay but He didn't give you the answers right away? Write about that experience here.

What situations have you been in that seemed dire at the onset but ended with a chance for God to be glorified when all was said and done? What situations are you in the middle of now that pose an opportunity for Jesus to be ultimately glorified?

_____

_____

_____

_____

_____

_____

_____

_____

_____

Have you ever struggled to know your purpose in life? Write a note to God, asking Him to reveal what He wants you to know about your individual purpose.

_____

_____

_____

_____

_____

_____

_____

_____

_____

_____

SCRIPTURE

"In the same way, you should be a light for other people. Live so that they will see the good things you do and will praise your Father in heaven."

MATTHEW 5:16 NCV

But the disciples, who were now in the middle of the lake, ran into trouble, for their boat was tossed about by the high winds and heavy seas. At about four o'clock in the morning, Jesus came to them, walking on the waves! When the disciples saw Him walking on top of the water, they were terrified and screamed, "A ghost!"
Then Jesus said, "Be brave and don't be afraid. I am here!"
Peter shouted out, "Lord, if it's really You, then have me join You on the water!"

"Come and join Me," Jesus replied. So Peter stepped out onto the water and began to walk toward Jesus. But when he realized how high the waves were, he became frightened and started to sink. "Save me, Lord!" he cried out.
Jesus immediately stretched out His hand and lifted him up and said, "What little faith you have! Why would you let doubt win?"
And the very moment they both stepped into the boat, the raging wind ceased. Then all the disciples bowed down before Him and worshiped Jesus. They said in adoration, "You are truly the Son of God!"

MATTHEW 14:24–33 TPT

PRAYER

Father, thank You for revealing to me the purpose of my existence. I want to glorify You with my actions, my words, my very being. I pray that when others see the good things I do, it would result in You alone being magnified. Forgive me when I have taken the glory for myself. It's all about You, and I realize that now. I praise You and give You the glory that You alone are due. God, I want my life to count for something, so please help me to let my light shine for You and not to be timid about it. Make me a city on a hill, salt and light, a lamp on the stand. Create in me good works to do even when I feel worn down or like things are too dire for me to even try. Energize me with Your goodness so I can point others to You. Jesus, as I walk beside You on this journey, help me to keep my eyes on You. Your ways are higher than mine, and even when I can't see how or why or when things will work out for Your glory, I trust that they will because I can take You at Your Word. In Your name, Amen.

Moment to Breathe

Take a moment to breathe in His Spirit and exhale out your uncertainty. Imagine you are outside walking on a park trail. You thought you could beat the rain despite what the weather app was forecasting, yet now you think differently as the sky turns gray and you can hear the rumble of thunder in the distance. The storm is coming, but oddly you feel at peace because you have been learning to rest in Jesus even in the midst of uncertainty. You have seen enough to know that storms are a part of life, but Jesus stands firm throughout them all. He tells you that the storm rolling in has the potential to cause some damage, but you need not fear because He is with you and will see you home in time. And even though you don't know how things will ultimately end, you do believe that you can take Jesus at His Word and that He is God even in the middle of a storm. Today you will rest in that truth. Take another deep breath in and receive your calm in the storm.

"Therefore everyone who hears these words of Mine and puts them into practice is like a wise man who built his house on the rock. The rain came down, the streams rose, and the winds blew and beat against that house; yet it did not fall, because it had its foundation on the rock." MATTHEW 7:24–25 NIV

REST AFTER A JOB WELL DONE

The apostles returned from their mission and gathered around Jesus and told Him everything they had done and taught. There was such a swirl of activity around Jesus, with so many people coming and going, that they were unable to even eat a meal. So Jesus said to His disciples, "Come, let's take a break and find a secluded place where you can rest a while." MARK 6:30–31 TPT

Once a person accepts Jesus as their Lord and Savior, their faith journey begins and so does the mission work. Over the course of life as a Christ follower, we will be given assignments to do in His name that will require service and sacrifice on our parts. Yet it is also rewarding to know that Jesus is a champion for our rest after a job well done.

The gospel of Mark records Jesus sending His apostles into Galilean villages where they were to preach, which they did with great success. But as they returned to inform Jesus of their adventures, they were swallowed up in the crowd. There was so much activity that they were not even able to eat a meal!

If you were in their sandals, after an extended journey, what would be your main priority? It probably would be the same as mine: to hug your loved ones, grab a bite to eat, and fall dramatically into your comfy bed while declaring, like Dorothy, "There's no place like home." But instead of that ideal homecoming, what if you find that your loved ones aren't there to greet you and you even can't get near your home because there is a swirl of activity going on in the streets? All you want is a hot meal and for your head to hit the pillow. Is that too much to ask?

How amazing would it be in that moment to know that Jesus sees your exhaustion and actually speaks right to your tired heart saying, *"Come, let's take a break and find a secluded place where you can rest a while."* Music to your ears, right?

When Jesus spoke these words to the disciples, He was speaking straight to their physical limitations and needs. The word *rest* in this passage means "to relax, to take a break from one's activities in order to be refreshed." He knew how hard they had been working. He knew the emotional, mental, and physical toil it took upon them to do the things He had asked them to do, and He discerned how important it would be for them to relax and be refreshed so they could recover for their next assignment.

Jesus recognizes that this is important for us too. He sees the work and the effort we are expending to grow His Kingdom. He doesn't ask us to do difficult things and not know the drain that comes with it. So He bids us to come and take a break so we can rest awhile and receive the refreshment we so desperately need.

Yes, to follow Jesus is serious work, but to steal some time away with Him to relax makes the labor worth it, and it's the very thing that keeps us going, so that when He sends us out again, we are well-rested and ready to receive our next assignment.

Reflection
- QUESTIONS -

The disciples were obedient to go when Jesus said to go and to come when He said to come, fully relying on Him to give them what they needed in terms of provision and rest. In what ways can you learn from their actions?

_____

_____

_____

_____

_____

_____

_____

_____

_____

_____

_____

_____

_____

_____

_____

_____

_____

_____

What is your ideal homecoming after a long business or ministry trip? In your own words, what does it mean "to be refreshed"? How can you find refreshment in a physical, emotional, and mental way? Now, what about a spiritual way?

_____

_____

_____

_____

_____

_____

_____

_____

Is there a "next assignment" to which you feel God may be calling you? How do you know when it's time to go versus when it's time to stay put?

_____

_____

_____

_____

_____

_____

_____

_____

SCRIPTURE

Then Joshua summoned the Reubenites, the Gadites and the half-tribe of Manasseh and said to them, "You have done all that Moses the servant of the LORD commanded, and you have obeyed me in everything I commanded. For a long time now—to this very day—you have not deserted your fellow Israelites but have carried out the mission the LORD your God gave you. Now that the LORD your God has given them rest as He promised, return to your homes in the land that Moses the servant of the LORD gave you on the other side of the Jordan."

JOSHUA 22:1–4 NIV

They were all worshiping the Lord and fasting for a certain time. During this time the Holy Spirit said to them, "Set apart for Me Barnabas and Saul to do a special work for which I have chosen them."
So after they fasted and prayed, they laid their hands on Barnabas and Saul and sent them out.

ACTS 13:2–3 NCV

May the favor of the Lord our God rest on us; establish the work of our hands for us— yes, establish the work of our hands.

PSALM 90:17 NIV

PRAYER

Jesus, thank You for being a champion for my physical rest after a job well done. It's a blessing to know that You see the physical, emotional, and mental toil it takes to perform with excellence. I appreciate You rewarding me with time to rest my body, mind, and spirit before going back at it. I know there are always things that threaten to keep me from resting, whether it be by my own doing or by the swirl of activity from others. Help me to safeguard the time You have given me to rest. Make it so I am intentional to steal away moments with You to gain the refreshment I need for my spirit. Delight me with Your refreshment like only You can do. Lord, when it's time for my next assignment, give me wisdom and discernment to know when to go and when to stay. I only want to go if You are in it, so let me know what things I should say "yes" to and which things I can say "no" to. You say to ask for wisdom, so I do just that. Be a fence around me today as I commit to rest in You. Amen.

Moment to Breathe

Take a moment to breathe in God's rest and exhale out your tiredness. Imagine yourself coming back from a long trip where there was much work to be done. You did it to the best of your ability and strived for excellence at every turn. You are ready to be home in your own bed, but for whatever reason, things keep popping up that are hindering you from making it there. Now imagine that Jesus is in the car with you. He tells you to pull over so that He can drive because He knows a fantastic spot where you can rest and recharge your body, mind, and spirit. You can't pull over fast enough! With Him at the steering wheel, you make it in record time to this place of refreshing and you find that your ideal homecoming is on full display. As your head hits the pillow, you hear Jesus whisper to you, "Rest, My daughter, after a job well done." Take one final deep breath in and receive your refreshment.

My whole being will be refreshed within me, and my bow will be renewed in my hand.
JOB 29:20 CSB

STUMBLING IN THE DARK

So when He heard that Lazarus was sick, He stayed where He was two more days, and then He said to His disciples, "Let us go back to Judea." "But Rabbi," they said, "a short while ago the Jews there tried to stone You, and yet You are going back?" Jesus answered, "Are there not twelve hours of daylight? Anyone who walks in the daytime will not stumble, for they see by this world's light. It is when a person walks at night that they stumble, for they have no light." JOHN 11:6–10 NIV

If you have ever found yourself in an unfamiliar place when the lights suddenly went out, you know it can be a disconcerting feeling. What once felt safe now may feel unsafe, and it could be that you are simultaneously trying to remember where the exit is and weighing the options of having your purse double as a weapon, should you need it. However, when the lights come back on, your eyes can normalize again, and hopefully your heart rate follows soon thereafter.

Light versus darkness is a common analogy that's easy to understand, which is precisely why Jesus used it so often in His teachings.

Stepping into the pages of Scripture again, we find that oddly enough, when Mary and Martha sent word to Jesus that the one He loved was sick (i.e., Lazarus), Jesus stayed where He was two more days. The disciples were not alarmed by this because Jesus had already told them that Lazarus's sickness would not result in death. But guess who wasn't privy to that conversation? That's right—Mary and Martha were back in Bethany sitting on pins and needles waiting for Jesus to show up in their time of need, yet He delayed another forty-eight hours. That's 172,800 seconds of praying that He was right around the corner, only to have their hopes of Lazarus making it out alive diminished with each passing hour. That is a dark place to be in. I know because I've been there.

When I was in my twenties, my brother was scheduled to stay with my husband and me while my parents were out of town. I was excited for the weekend and the fun that I had planned for us. But the weekend was over before it ever started because earlier that Friday afternoon, my brother was involved in a fatal car accident. However, I didn't know he had died on impact. All I knew was that there had been an accident. So, when I showed up to the hospital, I had braced myself that he was most likely badly hurt, but never in my wildest dreams did I believe he was dead. It wasn't even a possibility in my mind.

But then I was ushered into a private room, one typically reserved to deliver devastating news, and it was there that I was told that my hilarious, larger-than-life brother was dead. There was no hope that he could be revived. No time to even beg God for mercy. It was over. Final. He was only seventeen years old.

The days that followed were some of the darkest of my life, and it felt like Jesus was a long way off, never to return again. But that was just the darkness causing me to stumble. Because in reality, Jesus was right there with me. And He would never leave.

Reflection
- QUESTIONS -

Why do you think Scripture is filled with the idea of light contrasted with darkness? What does it teach you about God's nature?

Just as Mary and Martha sat in darkness, you have most likely had moments when you desperately needed Jesus to show up for you. Describe such a time below and record whether you felt His presence coming to dispel the darkness.

_____

_____

_____

_____

_____

_____

_____

_____

Why do you think God allows us to go through seasons of darkness? What purpose can be found in our pain, be it emotional, mental, or physical? What can we learn in these seasons?

_____

_____

_____

_____

_____

_____

_____

_____

SCRIPTURE

Because of God's tender mercy,
the morning light from heaven is
about to break upon us,
to give light to those who sit in
darkness and in the shadow of death,
and to guide us to the path
of peace.

LUKE 1:78–79 NLT

In the beginning was the Word, and
the Word was with God, and the
Word was God. He was with God in
the beginning. Through Him all things
were made; without Him nothing was
made that has been made. In Him
was life, and that life was the light of
all mankind. The light shines in the
darkness, and the darkness has not
overcome it.

JOHN 1:1–5 NIV

Where can I go from Your Spirit?
Where can I flee from Your presence?
If I go up to the heavens,
You are there;
if I make my bed in the depths,
You are there.
If I rise on the wings of the dawn,
if I settle on the far side of the sea,
even there Your hand will guide me,
Your right hand will hold me fast.
If I say, "Surely the
darkness will hide me
and the light become
night around me,"
even the darkness will
not be dark to You;
the night will shine like the day,
for darkness is as light to You.

PSALM 139:7–12 NIV

P R A Y E R

Jesus, oh, how I need You in my seasons of darkness. It feels awful to sit in the dark, watching the clock, wondering when You will come for me, but I know You are faithful and that You will come, just as You did for Mary and Martha. You say Your ways are higher than my ways and Your thoughts are higher than mine, so I will trust in Your sovereignty and believe that You will bring the light to my darkness. I know I am not called to sit in darkness forever, but I will wait on You so that I will not stumble. I know that You will lift me up and I will walk in the light of day again, so I wait for You to come. Come, Lord Jesus, with Your light and dispel the darkness that threatens to swallow me. Come like only You can and bring purpose to the pain. I need You now. Amen.

Moment to Breathe

Take a moment to breathe in His Spirit and exhale out your pain, whether it be emotional, mental, or physical. Imagine you are walking through a forest at dusk. Before you know it, the moonlight is covered by thick clouds, and you cannot see the path before you. As you try to feel your way around in the darkness, you stumble over logs, scratching yourself on the branches until you feel blood start to trickle down your limbs. You fall down completely before you finally give up trying to navigate through the darkness. But just as things seem totally hopeless, there is a flash of lightning! What you find is that with every flash of light, you can see what dangers are right in front of you. So you take a step and then wait for the next flash of lightning to come and dispel the darkness. Off in the distance, you can see what looks like a Man walking toward you. And in your heart, you know it won't be long now. Jesus is coming. So take a deep breath in and receive your flash of Light.

Yahweh is my revelation-light and the source of my salvation. I fear no one! I'll never turn back and run, for You, Yahweh, surround and protect me. PSALM 27:1 TPT

WALKING IN THE LIGHT

Finally, He said to His disciples, "Let's go back to Judea." But His disciples objected. "Rabbi," they said, "only a few days ago the people in Judea were trying to stone You. Are You going there again?" Jesus replied, "There are twelve hours of daylight every day. During the day people can walk safely. They can see because they have the light of this world. But at night there is danger of stumbling because they have no light." Then He said, "Our friend Lazarus has fallen asleep, but now I will go and wake him up." The disciples said, "Lord, if he is sleeping, he will soon get better!" They thought Jesus meant Lazarus was simply sleeping, but Jesus meant Lazarus had died. So He told them plainly, "Lazarus is dead. And for your sakes, I'm glad I wasn't there, for now you will really believe. Come, let's go see him." Thomas, nicknamed the Twin, said to his fellow disciples, "Let's go, too—and die with Jesus." JOHN 11:7–16 NLT

In the last entry, we felt the pain and distress of the sisters as they waited for Jesus to come and heal Lazarus, but as the minutes ticked by, the darkness settled like a thick cloud around them. They needed Him like parched land needs rain. Like a newborn baby needs milk. Like a fish needs water.

This was literally a "do-or-die situation." But there was also another matter that required attention. At this point in His ministry, Jesus had ruffled the feathers of the Pharisees to the point of them wanting Him gone—as in dead. The disciples knew the danger they would all be in if they returned to region of Judea, which encompassed Bethany, where Lazarus now lay dead. Jesus had told them that Lazarus's illness would not result in death and that he was now asleep. Perfect, right? If he was sleeping, then he'd feel better soon, and that way Jesus could continue on and not put all their lives in jeopardy by going to Bethany. But then Jesus told them plainly, "Lazarus is dead." So what is a faithful disciple to do besides relent like Thomas did and resolve to go with Jesus to Judea and be killed alongside Him? The disciples were most likely shaking their heads, wondering how things had gotten so dire in a hurry.

As we walk the path to Bethany with Jesus and the disciples, we are reminded once again that resting in Jesus does not equate to a life free from trouble, but rather it is choosing to trust Jesus in the midst of trouble. These were very serious challenges the disciples were facing, just as we have serious challenges we must face in our lives. But the way we can move forward with confidence is the same way Thomas did—by walking alongside the Light of the World.

Does that mean we won't endure seasons of darkness? Of course not. But what it does mean is that when we go through hardship (i.e., cancer treatment, a failed relationship, infertility/miscarriage, financial challenges, etc.), we walk through them differently than those who don't have a relationship with Jesus. Even as we walk through the valley of the shadow of death, just as the disciples were that day, we need not fear. Because where there is a shadow, Light is right around the corner!

Reflection
- QUESTIONS -

The apostle Thomas typically gets a bad rap as "Doubting Thomas," but here we see him as one who was willing to follow Jesus, even to the point of death. What can we as Christ followers learn from Thomas's example?

_____

_____

_____

_____

_____

_____

_____

_____

_____

_____

_____

_____

_____

_____

_____

_____

_____

Are you able to rest in Jesus even in the midst of today's serious challenges? Why or why not?

_____

_____

_____

_____

_____

_____

_____

_____

_____

_____

How have you personally been able to put into practice walking in light even in seasons of darkness? What hope can you offer the world?

_____

_____

_____

_____

_____

_____

_____

_____

_____

SCRIPTURE

"I am the light of the world. Anyone who follows Me will never walk in the darkness but will have the light of life."

JOHN 8:12 CSB

As He went along, He saw a man blind from birth. His disciples asked Him, "Rabbi, who sinned, this man or his parents, that he was born blind?" "Neither this man nor his parents sinned," said Jesus, "but this happened so that the works of God might be displayed in him. As long as it is day, we must do the works of Him who sent Me. Night is coming, when no one can work. While I am in the world, I am the light of the world."

JOHN 9:1–5 NIV

*He renews my life;
He leads me along the right paths
for His name's sake.
Even when I go through the
darkest valley,
I fear no danger,
for You are with me;
Your rod and Your staff—
they comfort me.*

PSALM 23:3–4 CSB

P R A Y E R

Jesus, You are the Light of the World, and in You there is no darkness! I hold on to this truth today and praise You for it. You have seen me through many serious challenges, and I know You will see me through the things I am facing today. Lord, I offer them to You now, believing that You will work them out for my good even if I can't see it in this moment. Thank You for the example of Thomas. Please give me the boldness to walk with You as he did. This is a faith journey, and I put my faith in the unshakable God. Forgive me when I doubt You are the God of my future. You know what it is that You have in store for me, so help me to trust You even when I can't see clearly. Pick me up when I stumble and fall. Place me on the path of light again. Help me to realize that even though things are dim, I can look for the shadow as I walk out my faith. Because where there is a shadow, there is always Light. Amen.

Moment to Breathe

Take a moment to breathe in God's rest and exhale out your fear of the future. Imagine that you are at the Grand Canyon. As you stand at the top of the National Park, you take in the breathtaking panoramic views. Witnessing the vastness of the canyon and the beauty of the different colors the rock takes on, you can't help but worship a God who could make something so magnificent. As you carefully peer over the side, you see people who are making their way up from the belly of the valley. Even though the sunlight is shining on you, those who are down in the valley are enveloped in darkness. You realize that you are both at the same Grand Canyon, surrounded by the same beauty, but that you are experiencing it in two completely different ways because of where you are in that moment. Yet, what you know that the person may not below, is that there is light on this side of the canyon and if they just keep the faith, the light will soon shine on them too. Take one more deep breath in and receive your enlightened perspective.

He shines a spotlight into caves of darkness, hauls deepest darkness into the noonday sun.
JOB 12:22 THE MESSAGE

EVEN NOW

When Jesus arrived, He found that Lazarus had already been in the tomb four days. Bethany was near Jerusalem (less than two miles away). Many of the Jews had come to Martha and Mary to comfort them about their brother. As soon as Martha heard that Jesus was coming, she went to meet Him, but Mary remained seated in the house. Then Martha said to Jesus, "Lord, if You had been here, my brother wouldn't have died. Yet even now I know that whatever You ask from God, God will give You." JOHN 11:17–22 CSB

What happens when all hope is lost? When even the remotest chance of realizing what you had hoped for has unmistakably vanished? And instead you are left with a gaping hole in your heart and possibly a crisis of faith. What if you have welcomed Jesus into your heart and home, sat at His feet, served His followers, and supported His ministry? And when you needed Him the most, He didn't come through for you? Does disappointment turn to bitterness and resentment? How could He leave you with a broken heart when you know for a fact that He has healed others and He even raised Jairus's daughter from the dead? But she was only dead for a little while, and your brother has been dead for four days—long enough to be past the point of no return. So the question remains, how will you respond when you finally do see Jesus again? Will you take the high road and let Him off the hook, because He probably was busy and forgot about your important message? Or do you let Him know how thoroughly let down and hurt you are?

This is the dilemma Mary and Martha found themselves in when suddenly word got to them that Jesus was near Bethany. Mary chose to sit while Martha couldn't get out the door fast enough—both responses accurately fitting their personalities.

Martha met Jesus on the road and uttered two statements: one filled with accusation and one filled with affirmation.

"Lord, if You had been here, my brother wouldn't have died. Yet even now I know that whatever You ask from God, God will give You."

Even now. Those two words are chock-full of meaning. Even now after four days of death. Even now that I've started the grieving process. Even now with all these people watching me. I will declare that I know You are capable of the impossible because I know who You are. You are the One who keeps hope alive.

Martha never was one to keep her thoughts to herself, so why start now? At the height of her crisis, she ushered forth her full faith in Jesus Christ as her Lord—not just because of what He can or could have done for her and Mary but because she truly believed He was the Son of God and that He could do whatever it was that the Father said He could do. Even now.

Reflection
- QUESTIONS -

Write about a time you stepped out in faith and welcomed Jesus into your heart and home, sat at His feet, served His followers, and even supported His ministry. And yet, when you needed Him the most, you felt as if He didn't come through for you.

If you were in Mary and Martha's situation, how do you think you would have responded when Jesus showed up after all hope was lost? Would you have run out to meet Him on the road or remained seated in the house? Write out your response below.

_____

_____

_____

_____

_____

_____

_____

_____

Do you believe Jesus is capable of impossible things? Why or why not? If you do believe, then finish this statement: Jesus, I know that because You are the Son of God, the Father will give You what You ask. So I ask that if it is Your will, even now that all hope seems lost, You will _____.

_____

_____

_____

_____

_____

_____

SCRIPTURE

*While Jesus was still speaking,
someone came from the house of
Jairus, the synagogue leader. "Your
daughter is dead," he said. "Don't
bother the teacher anymore."
Hearing this, Jesus said to Jairus,
"Don't be afraid; just believe,
and she will be healed."
When He arrived at the house of
Jairus, He did not let anyone go in
with Him except Peter, John and
James, and the child's father and
mother. Meanwhile, all the people
were wailing and mourning for her.
"Stop wailing," Jesus said.
"She is not dead but asleep."
They laughed at Him, knowing that
she was dead. But He took her by the
hand and said, "My child, get up!"
Her spirit returned, and at once
she stood up.*

LUKE 8:49–55 NIV

*"Whatever you ask in My name,
that will I do, so that the Father
may be glorified in the Son.
If you ask Me anything
in My name, I will do it."*

JOHN 14:13–14 NASB1995

*Now to Him who is able to do
immeasurably more than all we ask
or imagine, according to His power
that is at work within us, to Him be
glory in the church and in Christ Jesus
throughout all generations, for ever
and ever! Amen.*

EPHESIANS 3:20–21 NIV

PRAYER

Even now. This is a hard prayer to pray, Lord, especially when all hope seems lost. I thought You would come in time to spare me from my pain, but now I am left heartbroken, and I don't understand it at all. If You had been here, things would be different in this moment. I have faithfully followed You, but it doesn't seem like You care. Do You care, Jesus? I want to believe that You do still care, but I'm struggling with my faith right now. Can you please send Your angels to strengthen me? All I feel is my hopelessness. Bring me back to what I know is true about You. I know that You are the Son of God and that even now the Father will give You what You ask. I know that if it is Your will, You can do impossible things. I will rest in You and believe that, even now, You are still on Your throne. Amen.

Moment to Breathe

Take a moment to breathe in God's rest and exhale out your hopelessness. Imagine yourself sitting in an old church pew. The church is empty except for a few parishioners trickling in and out. They leave you alone to sob into your hands. You look to the altar and see the familiar cross on display, but instead of bringing you comfort, it only reminds you of your deep disappointment that He didn't come through for you. But then you see a glimmer of light as it shines on the stained glass. It tells the story of how there was an empty tomb and the angel declared, "He is not here. He has risen just as He said." It's then that you remember He is the God of the impossible. Even now, in your state of grief and pain, you still believe that He is who He says He is, and so you resolve to stand on that promise. With that in mind, take a deep breath in and receive your renewed hope.

My face has grown red with weeping, and darkness covers my eyes.... Even now my witness is in heaven, and my advocate is in the heights! JOB 16:16, 19 CSB

DO YOU BELIEVE?

Jesus said to her, "Your brother will rise again." Martha answered, "I know he will rise again in the resurrection at the last day." Jesus said to her, "I am the resurrection and the life. The one who believes in Me will live, even though they die; and whoever lives by believing in Me will never die. Do you believe this?" "Yes, Lord," she replied, "I believe that You are the Messiah, the Son of God, who is to come into the world." JOHN 11:23–27 NIV

Belief is a big deal to God—specifically, belief that Jesus Christ is the Son of God.

We can walk alongside Jesus, serve like Jesus, and have compassion like Jesus, but unless we believe in *who* Jesus is, we are just another good human. Our lives will come and go, and maybe a person or two will remember our earthly impact, but that will be as good as it gets. But if we truly believe Jesus is who He says He is, then that, my friend, is a game changer. Because not only will we be able to make an impact on this world while we are here, but we will also live forever. So, who exactly is Jesus, and why is it important to believe in Him? Let's join Jesus and Martha's conversation to find out the answer.

Martha had run out to meet Jesus on the street, where she simultaneously chastised Him for being late and clung to Him as her security. Jesus divulged to her what He had been telling the disciples: Lazarus, even though currently dead, would rise again. Martha, still clueless, responded with a theological statement tied to the Jewish teaching that at the last day, a resurrection would occur. Martha's hope was that both she and Lazarus would take part in that resurrection, but Jesus wanted her to look deeper. As the conversation switched from Lazarus's death to

what was to come spiritually, Jesus delivered one of the most glorious statements and concepts ever uttered to mankind.

"I am the resurrection and the life. The one who believes in Me will live, even though they die; and whoever lives by believing in Me will never die."

Jesus isn't just Lord over death; He is Lord over life! Yes, He takes the dead things and makes them alive again. But even more than that, He promises that even though we may die a physical death, our spirits will live on forever. This eternal life is available to everyone, but it comes with a question: *"Do you believe this?"*

Do you believe that Jesus is capable of resurrecting the dead? Do you believe that He Himself was resurrected? Do you believe that He defeated death? Do you believe that eternal life rests in Him? Do you believe that He is who He says He is?

As the Resurrection and the Life stared into Martha's eyes, did her eyes brim with tears of awe and respect as she responded in faith? *"Yes, Lord, I believe that You are the Messiah, the Son of God, who is to come into the world."*

He is the Anointed One, the Son of the Most High God. With Him, what seems like the end of life in the physical realm is only just beginning in the spiritual realm. He is the Resurrection and the Life.

Reflection

- Q U E S T I O N S -

Write about a time (or two) when you believed God would help you, and He did. (Maybe the "help" didn't look the way you wanted, but you know now that God was working it all out for your good.)

Why do you think belief is such a big deal to God? Why not just make eternal life available to us without our having to believe that Jesus is the Son of God?

_____

_____

_____

_____

_____

_____

_____

_____

_____

What are some "dead things" in your life that God is resurrecting? How does this help you to find rest in Jesus after experiencing Him as the Resurrection and the Life?

_____

_____

_____

_____

_____

_____

_____

_____

SCRIPTURE

Without faith it is impossible to please him, for whoever would draw near to God must believe that he exists and that he rewards those who seek him.

HEBREWS 11:6 ESV

"But about the resurrection of the dead—have you not read what God said to you, 'I am the God of Abraham, the God of Isaac, and the God of Jacob'? He is not the God of the dead but of the living."

MATTHEW 22:31–32 NIV

Jesus answered, "Truly, truly, I say to you, unless one is born of water and the Spirit he cannot enter into the kingdom of God. "That which is born of the flesh is flesh, and that which is born of the Spirit is spirit.

"Do not be amazed that I said to you, 'You must be born again.' "The wind blows where it wishes and you hear the sound of it, but do not know where it comes from and where it is going; so is everyone who is born of the Spirit." Nicodemus said to Him, "How can these things be?" Jesus answered and said to him, "Are you the teacher of Israel and do not understand these things?.... "As Moses lifted up the serpent in the wilderness, even so must the Son of Man be lifted up; so that whoever believes will in Him have eternal life. "For God so loved the world, that He gave His only begotten Son, that whoever believes in Him shall not perish, but have eternal life."

JOHN 3:5–16 NASB1995

P R A Y E R

Jesus, I declare that You are the Resurrection and the Life. You not only bring the dead things back to life, but You also offer eternal life. You are the Living God, and there is none like You. Thank You for showing me through Martha's eyes just how important it is to believe that You are who You say You are. Help me to see with spiritual eyes and not just in the natural. Ingrain in me the truth that even though I will die a physical death, I will not die a spiritual death, because I believe in You. Encourage me with this truth when my loved ones who believe in You pass away.

Thank You for allowing me to rest in You differently now that I have experienced You as the Resurrection and the Life. May my life be a reflection of this amazing grace. Amen.

Moment to Breathe

Take a moment to breathe in God's rest and exhale out the dead things in your life. Imagine that you are in a meeting room of recovering addicts of all kinds. You listen intently as, one by one, each person tells the story of how they were living a life that was not their own. They were chained to their addiction, a dead person walking. But then they tell of how they met Jesus and He offered to unchain them, but it came with a question: *"Do you believe that I am who I say I am?"* Those sitting in the room did believe, and they were resurrected back to life. Take another deep breath in and receive your own resurrection and new life.

Therefore, if anyone is in Christ, he is a new creation; the old has passed away, and see, the new has come! II CORINTHIANS 5:17 CSB

REST FOR YOUR HEALING IN TIMES OF GRIEF

Therefore, in order to keep me from becoming conceited, I was given a thorn in my flesh, a messenger of Satan, to torment me. Three times I pleaded with the Lord to take it away from me. But He said to me, "My grace is sufficient for you, for My power is made perfect in weakness." Therefore I will boast all the more gladly about my weaknesses, so that Christ's power may rest on me. That is why, for Christ's sake, I delight in weaknesses, in insults, in hardships, in persecutions, in difficulties. For when I am weak, then I am strong. II CORINTHIANS 12:7–10 NIV

Grief is a strange word. It's one of those words that gets stuck in your throat as you try to utter it. Even with its one syllable, it seems to drag out and sounds unpleasant to the ears. It's an even harder word to grab hold of, especially in a society where denial of grief is preferred. But the funny thing about grief is that if not dealt with, it will deal with you.

God made us with emotions, and to deny ourselves of feeling them is a travesty. Would we tell ourselves not to be happy on our wedding day? Should we force ourselves to not get excited when our dreams are realized? Of course not. So then, shall we not allow ourselves to feel saddened when loss occurs?

Actually, one of the most healing things we can do when our heart is hurting is to lean into that pain and acknowledge it. Because if we acknowledge it is real, then we can do something about it, which ideally would be to bring it to Jesus.

I remember feeling confused after the loss of my brother and even scared by my emotion as it pertained to Jesus. I was upset that He allowed such a loss to even occur, but I also needed Him like never before. I asked my Christian counselor about these conflicting feelings and admitted that I didn't know how to sort them out. He told me to bring every doubt, disappointment, and question to God because He is big enough to handle them all. He said, "In fact, April, God's power is made perfect in your weakness, so bring it all to Him." And as I did just that, I was able to not only lean into my grief but, more importantly, lean into my Savior. By simply resting in that place of vulnerability and honesty, I was learning to rest in Jesus.

Just as a physical wound needs time to scab over before it can stop bleeding, the same care must be taken with our hearts. We can't expect more of it than we do our own bodies. After the scab gives way, there will undoubtably be a scar, but if treated properly, even scars will fade in time. There will always be the hint of what was once a gaping hole, but the beautiful thing about scars is that they tell a story.

Grief provides us with the same opportunity. Once our pain eases and the healing comes and goes, we, too, will have a story to tell. A story about how resting in Jesus was the best ointment for our broken hearts.

Reflection
- QUESTIONS -

Grief can come over the loss of many things (i.e., the loss of a loved one, a marriage, a career, a home, or a dream). What losses have you experienced in your life that have resulted in a time of grieving? Is there anything you would do differently next time? Anything that worked well that you would like to repeat next time you are faced with loss?

Write about a time you tried push feelings of grief and sadness away. Then write about a time you chose to lean into your feelings and rest in Jesus.

What story do your scars tell, and how can you use them to help others who may be grieving?

SCRIPTURE

I cry aloud to the LORD;
I plead aloud to the LORD for mercy.
I pour out my complaint before Him;
I reveal my trouble to Him.

PSALM 142:1–2 CSB

"For My thoughts are
not your thoughts,
and your ways are not My ways."
This is the LORD's declaration.
"For as heaven is higher than earth,
so My ways are higher
than your ways,
and My thoughts than
your thoughts."

ISAIAH 55:8–9 CSB

He was despised and rejected—
a man of sorrows, acquainted
with deepest grief.
We turned our backs on Him and
looked the other way.
He was despised,
and we did not care.
Yet it was our weaknesses He carried;
it was our sorrows that
weighed Him down.
And we thought His troubles
were a punishment from God,
a punishment for His own sins!
But He was pierced for our rebellion,
crushed for our sins.
He was beaten so we could be whole.
He was whipped
so we could be healed.

ISAIAH 53:3–5 NLT

PRAYER

Lord, today I resolve to lean into my grief and pain and not dismiss it away. I know You understand my emotions because You are the One who created them, so I no longer will try to be "brave" and stuff down my feelings of hurt. By doing that, I am only hurting myself. Instead, I will bring You my pain and allow You to heal me from the inside out. Today my wound feels raw, but I know in time it will produce a scab that will give way to a scar. Help me to rest in You as I heal. Take my scars and use them for Your glory. Let me be willing to tell how You came and healed my broken heart—and how if You did it for me, You can do it for others in a similar situation. Ultimately, You heal all wounds, and time just helps. Help me to be patient in the healing. Be near, Jesus. I love and need You. Amen.

Moment to Breathe

Take a moment to breathe in God's rest and exhale out your grief and pain. Imagine that you are in the triage room at a hospital. There are several people sitting and waiting on their turn to see the doctor—some with big, gaping wounds, others with broken bones, and some with high fevers. People keep coming in at a rapid pace, each one unique in their need and pain. Your heart breaks for them even as you yourself sit wounded. But then the triage doors open, and you realize that the physician is Jesus Himself. He asks to see you for a moment. He says He knows that you need healing of your own, and He will be faithful to provide that, but He wonders if you wouldn't mind ministering to those in the waiting room who are going through the trauma of things you have dealt with in your past. You agree to this task, and as you show the other patients your healed scars, you find that you have moved back into a place of trust and rest. Because if He healed you once before, He can do it again. Take a final deep breath in and receive your healing balm.

Be merciful to me, LORD, for I am in distress; my eyes grow weak with sorrow, my soul and body with grief. But I trust in You, LORD, I say, "You are my God!" My times are in Your hands.
PSALM 31:9, 14–15 NIV

"FOR MY THOUGHTS

ARE NOT YOUR THOUGHTS,

AND YOUR WAYS ARE NOT MY WAYS."

THIS IS THE LORD'S DECLARATION.

"FOR AS HEAVEN IS

HIGHER THAN EARTH,

SO MY WAYS ARE HIGHER

THAN YOUR WAYS,

AND MY THOUGHTS

THAN YOUR THOUGHTS."

ISAIAH 55:8–9 CSB

COMFORTING OTHERS

Now Bethany was less than two miles from Jerusalem, and many Jews had come to Martha and Mary to comfort them in the loss of their brother. JOHN 11:18–19 NIV

Sometimes it's not the things we say that speak the loudest; it's the things that we do (or don't do) that make the most impact. In the South, we may not know what to say when someone dies, but we will bring you a casserole. It's not meant to be trite; it's meant to be comforting.

As someone who has seen my share of funerals, I often am asked to provide insight on how to comfort those who are grieving. Every so often, some typical excuses will make their way to my ears with statements like, "I'm afraid I'll say the wrong thing, so I'd better not say anything at all," or "They won't even know I'm there, so I'll just check in with them later." All of that may be true, but the fact is, when someone's world has just been turned upside down, they may not need you to say anything. They most likely just appreciate the fact that you are there in that moment—acknowledging their pain, holding space for them to be sad.

Mary and Martha had lost their brother, Lazarus—a devastating loss on all accounts. They had grown up together, sharing memories only they possessed. But also, since Scripture doesn't lead us to believe the sisters were married, Lazarus would have provided the covering that only a male in the household could. Without him, what did their future look like? Would they still be able to afford their home? Was their social standing in jeopardy? These were real perils of the day and age that Mary and Martha lived in.

However, it does seem as if the sisters had a good support system, as we are told that *"many Jews had come to Martha and Mary to comfort them in the loss of their brother."* These Jews were willing to put their own lives aside to come and mourn with these sisters, and they wept right alongside with them.

The apostle Paul gives these instructions in Romans 12:15 (CSB): "Rejoice with those who rejoice; weep with those who weep." These Jews were doing precisely that by comforting their friends, as Mary and Martha sought to get a grasp on what their new reality would entail. They, too, felt the sting of Lazarus's death and wept openly, just as they would soon rejoice with them.

Therein lies the beauty of holding space for our friends. Not every moment will be filled with weeping. There will be a cause to rejoice again. But in the occasion that their world has stopped when everyone else's keeps on spinning, it's a blessing to have those who will come over and not even say a word, but will just be sad with them. And who's to know when we may need the same comfort that only a true friend can provide?

Reflection

- Q U E S T I O N S -

Thinking about the loss of Lazarus from a first-century perspective, how does this impact how you view the seriousness of Mary and Martha's new reality? What other questions do you think were running through the sisters' minds as they pondered life without the covering Lazarus provided?

Describe in your own words what it means to "hold space" for someone. What are some specific examples of how you can both rejoice and weep with others?

The Jews put their lives on hold to come and sit with Mary and Martha. They were content to be in the same room and weep with them, and they didn't shy away from the pain death causes in the life of a loved one. Have you ever suffered a great loss yet experienced the comfort of your friends? Explain below.

WEEK 5 | DAY 1

SCRIPTURE

Rejoice with those who rejoice, and weep with those who weep.

ROMANS 12:15 NASB1995

All praises belong to the God and Father of our Lord Jesus Christ. For He is the Father of tender mercy and the God of endless comfort. He always comes alongside us to comfort us in every suffering so that we can come alongside those who are in any painful trial. We can bring them this same comfort that God has poured out upon us.

II CORINTHIANS 1:3–4 TPT

And we exhort you, brothers and sisters: warn those who are idle, comfort the discouraged, help the weak, be patient with everyone.

I THESSALONIANS 5:14 CSB

Now when Job's three friends heard of all this adversity that had come upon him, each one came from his own place—Eliphaz the Temanite, Bildad the Shuhite, and Zophar the Naamathite. For they had made an appointment together to come and mourn with him, and to comfort him. And when they raised their eyes from afar, and did not recognize him, they lifted their voices and wept; and each one tore his robe and sprinkled dust on his head toward heaven. So they sat down with him on the ground seven days and seven nights, and no one spoke a word to him, for they saw that his grief was very great.

JOB 2:11–13 NKJV

PRAYER

Lord, sometimes this life is hard, and there are real reasons for me to weep. Yet sometimes life is wonderful, and there are many reasons to rejoice. Thank You for giving me both experiences so I can know how others feel when they are going through times of sadness and happiness. When my friends go through difficult losses, let me be willing to put my life on hold to be there for them in their time of need. Take the feelings of inadequacy, discomfort, or inconvenience away from me, and help me to show up and hold space for them. Remind me in those moments that I needn't worry about what to say, I just need to hold space for their sadness and let You do the healing. Comfort them, Jesus, like only You can. I don't always understand, but I don't need to. I pray for them to see You in this situation, just like You have been faithful to be there for me in my darkest hours. I look to You, Jesus, as my Source of strength as I aim to be a comfort and a blessing to others. Amen.

Moment to Breathe

Take a moment to breathe in God's rest and exhale out your discomfort. Imagine that you are friends with the mother from the movie *Saving Private Ryan*. She has endured the unfathomable losses of three of her sons in World War II—each one of them awful in their own right. This is personal for you because you have witnessed these boys growing up with your own children. You don't have any words that will ease your friend's pain, but you are there, weeping right beside her. You fix her tea, you hand her tissues, and you simply hold space for her sadness. You call upon the name of the Lord to give you the strength to comfort her, and He does. You can feel Him near, so you pray fervently for your friend, as she does not have the strength to pray for herself. Then, many days later, you get word that your friend's only remaining son has been found, and he will be coming home from the war. You rejoice with your friend, grateful for the opportunity to hold this space of happiness and relief with her. So, take a deep breath in and receive your confidence to comfort others.

A friend loves you all the time, and a brother helps in time of trouble.
PROVERBS 17:17 NCV

YOUR HEART POSTURE

After she had said this, she went back and called her sister Mary aside. "The Teacher is here," she said, "and is asking for you." When Mary heard this, she got up quickly and went to Him. Now Jesus had not yet entered the village, but was still at the place where Martha had met Him. When the Jews who had been with Mary in the house, comforting her, noticed how quickly she got up and went out, they followed her, supposing she was going to the tomb to mourn there. When Mary reached the place where Jesus was and saw Him, she fell at His feet and said, "Lord, if You had been here, my brother would not have died." JOHN 11:28–32 NIV

Throughout Scripture, we find that what is of value to the world is of little value to God. He esteems things such as meekness, being gentle in spirit, showing mercy to others, and having a pure heart. He cares more about the posture of our hearts than He does our accomplishments, and we see evidence of this in living color through Mary's exchange with Jesus.

Let's return to the outskirts of Bethany, where Martha declared her belief in Jesus as the Messiah, the Son of God who has come into the world. After this faith-filled declaration, Jesus must have inquired about Mary, because Martha returned to their house and whispered to Mary, *"The Teacher is here and is asking for you."* At this one statement, Mary left the only posture we have known her to have—which is sitting—and hurried to where Jesus was.

What ran through Mary's mind as her feet took to the ground? Her Teacher, her Master, her Friend had asked for her to come, and so she came no questions asked. It was no longer time to sit. It was time to go to Jesus, with her heart broken but open to His mending.

When Mary reached Jesus and saw Him with her own eyes, her posture changed again. *"When Mary reached the place where Jesus was and saw Him, she fell at His feet and said, 'Lord, if You had been here, my brother would not have died.'"* Mary uttered the exact same sentence that Martha did earlier, but she said it from a different posture. She said this sentence at His feet—a place of submission, a place she considered fitting since He was her Master, and also a safe place to display her brokenness. It was a posture belonging to the pure of heart.

Jesus always wants us to come to Him with our brokenness, and He will never shame us for exactly how we come—whether we come like Martha, ready for a debate, or whether we come like Mary, ready for healing. But as we grow in our faith, what we find is that we can trust His heart, which in turn allows us to take on a heart posture that is fitting for the One we call "Lord."

This one sentence will be the only recorded words spoken by Mary in Scripture. But it never was Mary's words that spoke volumes anyhow—it was her consistent heart posture. May the same be true of us.

Reflection
- QUESTIONS -

Mary and Martha had their individual moments with Jesus in which they came to Him with their brokenness when they just as easily could have avoided Him. In what ways have you been known to bring your brokenness to Jesus like Martha? In what ways have you been like Mary? In what ways have you chosen to avoid bringing Jesus your pain?

How can you trust Jesus's heart even during times of pain? Does trusting Him with your brokenness alter your heart posture? Explain why or why not.

_____

_____

_____

_____

_____

_____

_____

_____

_____

Right now, if you are able, place yourself into a physical posture of submission before the Lord. Tell Him what is on your mind, and then record here what you feel His Spirit is whispering back to you.

_____

_____

_____

_____

_____

_____

_____

_____

SCRIPTURE

Blessed are the poor in spirit,
for theirs is the kingdom of heaven.
Blessed are those who mourn,
for they will be comforted.
Blessed are the meek,
for they will inherit the earth.
Blessed are those who hunger and
thirst for righteousness,
for they will be filled.
Blessed are the merciful,
for they will be shown mercy.
Blessed are the pure in heart,
for they will see God.

MATTHEW 5:3–8 NIV

Therefore, submit to God. Resist the
devil, and he will flee from you. Draw
near to God, and He will draw near
to you. Cleanse your hands, sinners,
and purify your hearts, you double-
minded. Be miserable and mourn and
weep. Let your laughter be turned
to mourning and your joy to gloom.
Humble yourselves before the Lord,
and He will exalt you.

JAMES 4:7–10 CSB

For with the heart one believes
and is justified, and with the mouth
one confesses and is saved. For
the Scripture says, "Everyone who
believes in Him will not be
put to shame."

ROMANS 10:10–11 ESV

P R A Y E R

Jesus, You are still my Lord and Master, even in the middle of my brokenness. My heart cries out to You from a posture of submission. I believe like Martha that You are the Messiah, the Son of God who has come into the world. I trust like Mary that Your heart is for me and that You will heal me as You have been faithful to do in the past. I bring to You everything that is causing me pain in this moment, and I surrender it to You all over again, knowing that with You is where my healing is. Forgive me for the times that I came to You with the wrong heart posture or when I avoided You altogether, thinking that You were no longer worth coming to. Thank You for receiving me even though I didn't behave as I now know that I should. You never shamed me, and I am so grateful. Bring to mind Mary's example the next time that I am faced with a similar situation, and let me move toward you with swiftness and purpose as I fall at Your feet. You are God over it all, and You are the Lord of my life. I love You, Jesus. Amen

Moment to Breathe

Take a moment to breathe in God's rest and exhale out your brokenness. See yourself sitting in a field of sunflowers. The brightness of them doesn't match your dark mood, but you are grateful for them nonetheless, because they remind you that one day the sun will shine on you like that again. You're not quite sure how long you've been sitting here, but it has been long enough for you to do some deep soul-searching. Suddenly, you hear your name being called. As you look up, you squint to see a figure in front of the light, and He is asking for you to come to Him. You know His voice, so you hurry through the fields so that you can get to Him. When you make it to your Teacher, you fall at His feet and hand Him your broken heart. He lovingly takes it into the palm of His hands and lifts you up again. For the first time in a long time, you know that you are going to be okay. Take one more deep breath in and receive your restoration.

He heals the wounds of every shattered heart. PSALM 147:3 TPT

JESUS WEEPS TOO

When Jesus saw her weeping, and the Jews who had come along with her also weeping, He was deeply moved in spirit and troubled. "Where have you laid him?" He asked. "Come and see, Lord," they replied. Jesus wept. Then the Jews said, "See how He loved him!" But some of them said, "Could not He who opened the eyes of the blind man have kept this man from dying?"
JOHN 11:33–37 NIV

There's something so satisfying about a good thunderstorm, especially after a long, hot summer day. It's as if God Himself has held back His emotions for long enough, and then He finally allows the skies to pour down rain like thick drops of tears, and the thunder to bellow out all that He has been holding back. Once it all passes, the grass is greener and the flowers stand taller. Somehow it was necessary, terrible, and wonderful all at the same time.

There is comfort in knowing that the God of all creation experiences the same human emotions we do, and no story conveys this better than the one we are walking with Mary and Martha. We are told that when Jesus saw Mary and her friends weeping, He was "deeply moved in spirit and troubled." Jesus was upset over the death of Lazarus and the pain it was causing those He loved. And even though He knew Lazarus was about to come walking out of that grave, in that moment, when He felt the crushing sting of death, something had to break. So, Jesus wept. He wept for Mary and Martha, and He wept for Himself. And He weeps for you and me too.

The night my brother died, I curled up on my bed in a fetal position. I felt like a rubber band had been placed around my heart, and with every beat, the life was being squeezed out of it. I didn't know how I would survive the days to come or if I even wanted to survive them. I was reeling from the unfairness of it all. But I wasn't alone that night, because Jesus was there holding me and was weeping too. His heart was shattered just like mine was, and He hated the sting of death even more than I did. Never once did He let go, even if I couldn't perceive it in the days to come. He wept with me and for me.

We are promised by God Himself that there will be a day when there will be no more death, no more suffering, no more cancer or illness, no more suicide, no more eating disorders, no more miscarriages or stillborn births, no more grief, and no more pain. Jesus will come back for His bride, which is the church, and when He does, He will defeat death once and for all. And when He does, He promises to wipe away every tear from our eyes.

Our tears matter to Jesus. He is not a cold, uncaring God. Quite the opposite, in fact. We can rest assured that when those whom He loves feel pain, He feels it as well, and He is right there with us, weeping too.

Reflection
- QUESTIONS -

What does it mean for you to know that Jesus, even though He is God, weeps? Does it change your perspective of Him or deepen your admiration of Him? Explain.

When Jesus comes back for His church and defeats death once and for all, what "no more" of are you most looking forward to and why?

During your times of resting in Jesus thus far, have you felt as if your tears matter to Him? Are there tears you have been holding back and need to release to Him now? Allow Him to weep with you here.

SCRIPTURE

Then I saw a new heaven and a new earth, for the first heaven and the first earth had passed away, and the sea was no more. And I saw the holy city, new Jerusalem, coming down out of heaven from God, prepared as a bride adorned for her husband. And I heard a loud voice from the throne saying, "Behold, the dwelling place of God is with man. He will dwell with them, and they will be his people, and God himself will be with them as their God. He will wipe away every tear from their eyes, and death shall be no more, neither shall there be mourning, nor crying, nor pain anymore, for the former things have passed away."

REVELATION 21:1–4 ESV

For God, who said, "Let light shine out of darkness," made His light shine in our hearts to give us the light of the knowledge of God's glory displayed in the face of Christ. But we have this treasure in jars of clay to show that this all-surpassing power is from God and not from us. We are hard pressed on every side, but not crushed; perplexed, but not in despair; persecuted, but not abandoned; struck down, but not destroyed.

II CORINTHIANS 4:6–9 NIV

You have recorded my troubles. You have kept a list of my tears. Aren't they in Your records?

PSALM 56:8 NCV

PRAYER

Jesus, how do I even begin to understand the depth of Your emotion? How reassuring it is to know that I serve a God who loves me and who weeps when I weep. You are not a cold, uncaring God. You are compassionate and tenderhearted. Your heart breaks when mine does, and You love me through it all. Thank You for never leaving me to face my grief and pain alone. You were there, holding me, weeping with me, letting me know You care. Even when I couldn't feel anything but the loss, never once did You leave my side. I praise You in advance for the day when death is defeated once and for all and there is no more grief, no more crying, and no more pain. What a day that will be! Come soon, Jesus. Until then, love me like only You can and help me rest in You. Amen.

Moment to Breathe

Take a moment to breathe in God's rest and exhale out your tears. Imagine you are on a back porch sitting in a rocking chair. The air is thick with humidity, and you can hear the thunder getting a little louder and more menacing with each boom. Before long the sky opens up and the rain begins to pour, as you knew it most certainly would. No cloud could contain that amount of moisture. As you rock back and forth, listening to the thunder and the rain, you find that tears are rolling down your cheeks. The release of them feels necessary and terrible and wonderful all at the same time. You look over to where sits Jesus in the rocking chair right next to you. Tears are streaming down His cheeks as well, and He reaches over and takes your hand. You realize He was there all along, and never once did He leave or forsake you. With that in mind, take a deep breath in and receive your assurance that He sees every single one of your precious tears.

He made darkness His canopy around Him—the dark rain clouds of the sky. Out of the brightness of His presence bolts of lightning blazed forth. The LORD thundered from heaven; the voice of the Most High resounded. II SAMUEL 22:12–14 NIV

IT'S TIME TO TAKE OFF
THE GRAVE CLOTHES

Jesus, once more deeply moved, came to the tomb. It was a cave with a stone laid across the entrance. "Take away the stone," He said. "But, Lord," said Martha, the sister of the dead man, "by this time there is a bad odor, for he has been there four days." Then Jesus said, "Did I not tell you that if you believe, you will see the glory of God?" So they took away the stone. Then Jesus looked up and said, "Father, I thank You that You have heard Me. I knew that You always hear Me, but I said this for the benefit of the people standing here, that they may believe that You sent Me." When He had said this, Jesus called in a loud voice, "Lazarus, come out!" The dead man came out, his hands and feet wrapped with strips of linen, and a cloth around his face. Jesus said to them, "Take off the grave clothes and let him go." JOHN 11:38–44 NIV

Before we come to the unforgettable conclusion of the story we've been engrossed in for these past few weeks, we see one last exchange between Martha and her Master. As Jesus ordered the stone to be taken away, Martha spoke up again, now wearing the label of "the dead man's sister." Martha objected to Jesus's instruction, noting that after four days of being dead Lazarus surely "stinketh" (see KJV). Oh, Martha, ever the literalist.

It's somewhat easy to judge Martha for her critical lapse in faith, but when you are staring at a closed grave and the reality is that the body behind it reeks (not to mention it's the body of someone you love), it's easy to lose sight of the bigger picture. But even now, Jesus brings it right back to believing in Him and once more states the purpose of Lazarus's death. Remember, it's all about who gets the glory, and the Father will be glorified!

After Jesus prayed, He called out in a loud voice, "Lazarus, come out!" And lo and behold, the dead man, a man whose soul had no hope of returning to his body, a man who surely stinketh, comes walking out of that grave. What was the reaction of our beloved sisters? Did they gasp in disbelief? Did they hug each other tightly as Lazarus came closer? Did they fall to their knees at Jesus's feet in adoration and deep gratitude? Did they rush to unbind Lazarus, kissing his face and wetting it with their tears of unbridled joy?

Jesus was probably smiling to Himself as He witnessed their range of emotions, and from what we know about Jesus, He probably had some emotions of His own. The Father did, indeed, hear Jesus's prayer, and there would be much commotion in the days to come over such a scene, but for now, there was one last instruction to give as it pertained to Lazarus, *"Take off the grave clothes and let him go."*

However, in the end, it wasn't just Lazarus who needed to be untied of the grave clothes. Mary and Martha were no longer the "sisters of the dead man." The one whom both they and Jesus loved had been resurrected back to life, and that label was no longer appropriate. As their own hearts began to beat again, they would have to let go of the former things, which required them to take off their own grave clothes and forsake a label they were currently wearing. They had been redeemed.

Reflection
- QUESTIONS -

Have you ever personally experienced or observed a miracle? Write about how God showed up in an amazing way in your life, and praise Him for it.

What dead labels have you worn in your lifetime, either willingly or unwillingly? Have you been able to experience being set free from them? Tell how below.

_____

_____

_____

_____

_____

_____

_____

_____

_____

_____

What does it mean to live as a woman who is redeemed? How does being a redeemed woman of God differ from being a perfect woman?

_____

_____

_____

_____

_____

_____

_____

_____

_____

_____

SCRIPTURE

"Do not fear,
for I have redeemed you;
I have summoned you by name;
you are Mine.
When you pass through the waters,
I will be with you;
and when you pass
through the rivers,
they will not sweep over you.
When you walk through the fire,
you will not be burned;
the flames will not set you ablaze.
For I am the LORD your God,
the Holy One of Israel, your Savior;

ISAIAH 43:1–3 NIV

GOD brings death and GOD brings life,
brings down to the grave
and raises up.

I SAMUEL 2:6 THE MESSAGE

At last we have freedom, for Christ
has set us free! We must always
cherish this truth and firmly refuse to
go back into the bondage
of our past.

GALATIANS 5:1 TPT

P R A Y E R

Oh, Jesus, what an epic ending! Only You could have pulled off such a feat. To bring a man who had been in the grave for four days back to life is simply unheard of, but You are the God of the impossible. You are the One who brings dead things back to life. You are the One who holds the power of life, and at the command of Your voice, everything has to obey, even the grip of death on a man who surely stinketh. Thank You for what You have taught me as I've walked with Mary and Martha through the death and resurrection of their brother. It wasn't easy, but it was worth it.

Lord, just like Martha, I am quick to get comfortable in certain labels that I don't need to wear. Redeem them from me. Let me forget the former things and look forward to the future that You have in store for me. If there is anything holding me back, reveal it to me now. Let me come walking out of that grave so that I can give You the glory once again. I love You, Lord. Amen.

Moment to Breathe

Take a moment to breathe in God's rest and exhale out any dead labels that you have been wearing. Imagine you are at the movie theater, where you have been engrossed in a dramatic movie for the past hour and a half with your tub of hot, buttery popcorn. The film ends with a climactic ending where the Hero saves the day and mankind, much to everyone's excitement and relief. But before the credits start rolling, the actors and actresses in the film are lined up and wearing T-shirts with various labels on them. *Adulterer. Anger Issues. Bad Mom.* And the list goes on. Then the Hero returns and He gives them new T-shirts to wear. The new shirts are bright white with one word stamped across them: *REDEEMED*. The Hero is offering these shirts to the audience as well, but He gives the instruction that if you take one, you cannot wear your old label any longer. You think about it for a moment and then decide you would rather trade your label for a *REDEEMED* shirt. You walk out of the movie theater wearing your new shirt, feeling freer than you have ever been. Take another deep breath in and receive your unbridled joy.

My lips will shout for joy when I sing praise to You because You have redeemed me.
PSALM 71:23 CSB

RESTING THROUGH PRAYER

"So it is with your prayers. Ask and you'll receive. Seek and you'll discover. Knock on heaven's door, and it will one day open for you. Every persistent person will receive what he asks for. Every persistent seeker will discover what he needs. And everyone who knocks persistently will one day find an open door. Let Me ask you this: Do you know of any father who would give his son a snake on a plate when he asked for a serving of fish? Of course not! Do you know of any father who would give his daughter a spider when she had asked for an egg? Of course not! If imperfect parents know how to lovingly take care of their children and give them what they need, how much more will the perfect heavenly Father give the Holy Spirit's fullness when His children ask Him." LUKE 11:9–13 TPT

One of the beautiful things about being a Christ follower is that we have access to the Father. This is monumental, because had Jesus not presented Himself as the spotless Lamb of God, we wouldn't be able to pray to Him ourselves. We would have to bring our sacrifice to the temple and ask the priest to intercede on our behalf. Thank goodness the work has already been done and we can talk to God anytime we want!

But what if we took this amazing gift that we have been given and we didn't use it? Think about it this way: imagine you were generously given the keys to your dream car, right down to the perfect color, make, and model. But instead of immediately taking it for a spin, you said, "I'm too nervous to drive it today, so I'm going to park it, and maybe tomorrow I'll be ready." But tomorrow comes and goes, and you still don't get behind the wheel. Next thing you know, a month has passed and then another. Every time you walk past your car, there is a twinge of guilt that you aren't using it, but by now you've gotten used to walking around it. And so it sits until it gets old and rusty. What a shame! Imagine the adventures you could have had in it. Sure, it might have gotten a few dings and scrapes on it, but all in all, it's a vehicle that was meant to be driven, not parked.

The same is true of our prayer life. God doesn't require us to pray in a perfect manner or to be perfect in order to pray. He just wants us to come and talk to Him, bringing Him our big things and small things, our achievements and failures, our hopes for the future and our day-to-day activities. He wants it all. And the best part is that He promises to hear us when we pray.

Right before Jesus called Lazarus's name to come out of the grave, He looked up and prayed this prayer: *"Father, thank You for hearing me. You always hear me, but I said it out loud for the sake of all these people standing here, so that they will believe You sent Me"* (John 11:41–42 NLT). What a significant affirmation given by the Son to His Father, which was reciprocated with Jesus receiving exactly what He asked.

Therein lies the gift to us. As we rest in Jesus, we find that we can pray with confidence only because of His sacrifice. We don't have to get it perfect, we just have to do it—resting in the assurance that we will be heard by the Almighty. So, what do you say? Let's crank up the ignition and give our gift of prayer a spin.

Reflection
- QUESTIONS -

When Jesus prayed, He often looked up. Why do you think He did this? Also, Jesus regularly went off by Himself to pray to the Father. If it was necessary for Jesus to pray, how much more necessary is prayer in your own life?

Being honest with yourself—on a scale of 1 to 10, where do you think your prayer life falls? List one or two practical things you can do to improve this score.

Throughout this walk with Mary and Martha, in what ways has prayer helped you (or not helped you) rest in Jesus?

S C R I P T U R E

Therefore, brothers and sisters, since we have confidence to enter the Most Holy Place by the blood of Jesus, by a new and living way opened for us through the curtain, that is, His body, and since we have a great priest over the house of God, let us draw near to God with a sincere heart and with the full assurance that faith brings, having our hearts sprinkled to cleanse us from a guilty conscience and having our bodies washed with pure water.

HEBREWS 10:19–22 NIV

Be devoted to prayer, keeping alert in it with thanksgiving.

COLOSSIANS 4:2 LEB

When a believing person prays, great things happen. Elijah was a human being just like us. He prayed that it would not rain, and it did not rain on the land for three and a half years! Then Elijah prayed again, and the rain came down from the sky, and the land produced crops again.

JAMES 5:16–18 NCV

I call on You, my God,
for You will answer me;
turn Your ear to me
and hear my prayer.
Show me the wonders
of Your great love,
You who save by Your right hand
those who take refuge in You
from their foes.
Keep me as the apple of Your eye;
hide me in the shadow of Your wings.

PSALM 17:6–8 NIV

P R A Y E R

Father, what a gift it is to have access to You! Thank You, Jesus, for Your sacrifice that makes it possible for me to pray to the Father. I stand in awe that You would do that for me, and I ask that You help me not to take the gift of prayer for granted. Forgive me for the times when I have forfeited my gift, thinking that my prayers didn't matter or that if I didn't pray "perfectly" I might as well not even do it at all. I know You want me to bring You everything—big or small—because that's the kind of God You are. You just want to have a relationship with me. So today I look up with confidence, knowing that You hear me and that You will give me what I ask of You in Jesus's name as it pertains to Your glory. Rid me of my selfish ambitions or my laziness as it relates to my prayer life. Energize me to want to keep our communication vibrant as well as respectful. There is none like You, and I give You all the honor and praise. Hear my prayer, O Lord. In Jesus's wonderful name, amen.

Moment to Breathe

Take a moment to breathe in God's rest and exhale out your timidness as it pertains to prayer. It's Christmas morning, and you are a young girl again, ready to see which gifts bear your name underneath the tree. You see one wrapped in gold paper with a bright red bow on it, and you hope that one is yours. As your family takes turns unwrapping gifts, your Father goes to the tree and picks up the shiny gift. He makes his way toward you and says that He bought this gift especially for you and He can't wait for you to open it. But suddenly, you feel nervous rather than excited about opening it. What if you don't enjoy it to the level that you think your Father wants you to? So you reluctantly tell Him to give your gift to someone else. Ahh, but your Father knows you better than you know yourself, and at His gentle prodding, you finally unwrap your gift. There you find it is exactly what you have wanted and needed all this time, and you can't wait to grow old with it as a part of your life. Take a final deep breath in and receive your access to the Father.

But each day the LORD pours His unfailing love upon me, and through each night I sing His songs, praying to God who gives me life. PSALM 42:8 NLT

A SHIFT IN PERSPECTIVE

Six days before the Passover, Jesus came to Bethany, where Lazarus lived, whom Jesus had raised from the dead. Here a dinner was given in Jesus' honor. Martha served, while Lazarus was among those reclining at the table with Him. Then Mary took about a pint of pure nard, an expensive perfume; she poured it on Jesus' feet and wiped His feet with her hair. And the house was filled with the fragrance of the perfume. JOHN 12:1–3 NIV

Dear friend, it's hard to believe we have come to the final stretch of our walk with Mary and Martha. We have kept in step with these two sisters, learning how to rest in Jesus even if our circumstances are less than ideal. He is so faithful, after all, and to rest in Him is right where we are meant to be.

But before we hug and say goodbye, we have one last week with Mary and Martha, and it's a good one. We return to the place where we first met them, and again there is a dinner being served. Everyone is in their rightful places, but this time the sisters are in a different state of mind. There is a spirit of gratitude and thanksgiving where there once was resentment and comparison.

As we join our friends in Bethany, we are given the information the Passover will soon take place. As Christ followers, we know this means that Jesus will begin making His way to the cross to die for our sins and will be resurrected three days later, but Mary and Martha don't have that privilege. They are going to have to live it out, resting in Jesus all over again. However, tonight they are hosting a dinner in Jesus' honor. Martha resumes her service to Jesus, operating in her gift of hospitality, and we find that she is no longer serving out of frustration to get the meal prepped

but out of a place of deep gratitude and reverence to bring her best offering to Jesus. This time she is content to let Mary be where she is supposed to be, which is once again at Jesus's feet.

There is something so tender about the way that Scripture simply states the sisters' whereabouts during the dinner, as if their redeemed status has enhanced their gifting, making Martha's ability to serve and Mary's willingness to be at Jesus's feet even sweeter. It seems as if this was how it was supposed to be all along. It took a long and winding road to get there, but they are there, serving and sitting. Each beautiful and necessary in her own right. Each bringing honor to Jesus.

When Jesus shines His light and heals our brokenness, our perspective shifts. And when our perspective shifts, things that were once mundane, like daily activities, become acts of service before a holy God. Material things that were once important no longer carry the same weight. Arguments that were once justified now just seem petty. Our focus becomes more eternity-minded because we have captured a glimpse of the deep things of God. We are changed for the better and have learned what it truly means to rest in our Savior.

Reflection
- QUESTIONS -

The gospel of John places this dinner inside what we know of as Passion Week, meaning that Jesus's earthly ministry was rapidly coming to an end. How does knowing what will soon transpire deepen your appreciation for Mary and Martha in this moment in history? Explain below.

_____

_____

_____

_____

_____

_____

_____

_____

_____

_____

_____

_____

_____

_____

_____

_____

_____

_____

Mary and Martha are seen operating in their strengths and their callings at this dinner for Jesus, demonstrating a spirit of gratitude for what Jesus did for them. Describe how your calling has been strengthened over these past few weeks as you have learned to rest in Jesus. How has your perspective shifted for the better?

_____

_____

_____

_____

_____

_____

_____

In your own words, what does it mean to be "eternity minded"? Share below some specific ways in which you plan to implement this way of living from here on out.

_____

_____

_____

_____

_____

_____

_____

_____

_____

SCRIPTURE

When it was almost time for the Jewish Passover, many went up from the country to Jerusalem for their ceremonial cleansing before the Passover. They kept looking for Jesus, and as they stood in the temple courts they asked one another, "What do you think? Isn't He coming to the festival at all?" But the chief priests and the Pharisees had given orders that anyone who found out where Jesus was should report it so that they might arrest Him.

JOHN 11:55–57 NIV

Therefore I, the prisoner in the Lord, urge you to walk worthy of the calling you have received, with all humility and gentleness, with patience, bearing with one another in love, making every effort to keep the unity of the Spirit through the bond of peace.

EPHESIANS 4:1–3 CSB

Therefore, since we are receiving a kingdom that cannot be shaken, let us be thankful. By it, we may serve God acceptably, with reverence and awe, for our God is a consuming fire.

HEBREWS 12:28–29 CSB

P R A Y E R

Dear Jesus, I come before You today with a spirit of gratitude and thankfulness for all You have done in my life. Just like Mary and Martha, I invite You all over again into my heart and home so that I can both serve You and sit with You. Thank You for teaching me how to operate in my strengths and my calling and to put aside petty disputes and inconsequential things. I truly have felt the shift in my perspective over these past few weeks, and I no longer look at things in the same light as I did before. I am more eternity-minded because of the time I have spent with You—believing in You, trusting in You, and resting in You. The next time trials and temptations arise, help me to remember this shift in perspective and how You healed me and called me Yours. I see more clearly who I truly am in You. So now, in this moment and with a grateful heart, I give honor where honor is due. Jesus, it's all about You. It always has been, and it always will be. Amen.

Moment to Breathe

Take a moment to breathe in God's rest and exhale out your former perspective. Imagine that you are at your favorite restaurant with all your favorite people. You are sitting at a round table, and as you intentionally look into the eyes of each one of them, you praise God for placing them in your life. Sure, there have been rocky times and even some sharp disagreements, but you now see things differently, and those things that were once important seem minor now. After the main course is over, you study the dessert menu, knowing it will be hard to choose just one. But before you even have a chance to order, the server appears with one of every dessert on the menu and a plethora of spoons so you and your friends can share. As you pass around the platter, you can't help smiling across the table at the One who made this all possible. Finally, you can't hold back your thankfulness any longer, and you find yourself at His feet again, which is right where you are supposed to be. So, take a deep breath in and receive your spirit of gratitude.

Give thanks to the LORD, for He is good. His love endures forever. Give thanks to the God of gods. His love endures forever. Give thanks to the Lord of lords: His love endures forever.
PSALM 136:1–3 NIV

POUR YOUR LOVE ON JESUS

Then Mary took about a pint of pure nard, an expensive perfume; she poured it on Jesus' feet and wiped His feet with her hair. And the house was filled with the fragrance of the perfume.
JOHN 12:3 NIV

What happens inside the soul of a woman when she is given the desires of her heart? What lengths will she go to in order to express her thankfulness?

Mary knew how awful it felt to sit in darkness, and she knew how glorious it was to bask in the light of day. She couldn't hold back her love for Jesus, so she came to dinner with a gift in hand. And not just any gift but an extravagant one. One that cost her a great deal—a year's worth of wages, to be exact. But to her, the cost was worth it, because to have Lazarus back among the living was worth any amount of money.

The gospel of Mark tells us that Mary came with an alabaster jar of very expensive perfume, made of pure nard, and that she broke the jar when she was ready to anoint Jesus. Alabaster is a hard white stone. It was the container of choice to hold valuable spices and oils because of its ability to preserve and protect them. Spikenard comes from rare plants in the land of India and was used to anoint the body of a loved one at their burial. Because of its cost, a family would save this perfume for such an occasion, because once the alabaster jar was broken open, it must be used in its entirety.

When Mary broke the alabaster jar, the aroma of the spikenard would have permeated the entire home. And there was to be only one recipient of such a gift, her Lord and Master. As Mary poured the pure nard onto Jesus's head and watched it trickle down His beard, she loosened her hair and found herself once again at Jesus's feet. With the remaining perfume, she anointed His feet and wiped them with her hair, which most certainly would have attracted the attention of every single person in the room.

Despite the undoubtedly gaping jaws of every other dinner guest at her extravagant gesture, their presence simply faded into the background. The room transformed into a sanctuary with only her and her Lord. Mary was unabashed as she intentionally poured out every ounce of love she had onto the Son of God in the most beautiful and humble of ways.

When Jesus surpasses being the Person whom we pray to when we're in a jam, or even a good Teacher or Friend to us, and becomes our everything, it's then that we fall to our knees in adoration and bring Him our very best gift. We risk being ridiculed by others for letting down our hair and wiping Jesus's feet, but we don't stop, because our eyes aren't on them. Our eyes are on our greatest delight. His name is Jesus.

Reflection
- QUESTIONS -

Both the alabaster jar and the spikenard were costly in their own right. The only way to get to the perfume was to break the jar, meaning that both the perfume and the jar could not be used ever again. With a better understanding of how Mary's gift differs from our twenty-first-century perfumes, does this change the way you view her sacrifice? Would you have been willing to pour out a year's worth of wages onto Jesus? Why or why not?

Mary's anointing of Jesus is considered to be an act of worship. List two examples of how we as women can worship Jesus in a similar manner with a gift that is both extravagant and intentional, knowing that it's not so much about the dollar sign that gets Jesus's attention, but rather the sacrifice.

Jesus can be many things to us, ranging from Mighty God to Prince of Peace and different things in between, depending on the season of life we are in. Yet as we grow in our faith, so does our view of who Jesus is. It's when He becomes our everything that we respond with worship. In the space below, take a minute to tell Jesus where you see Him in this season and ask for Him to continue to reveal Himself to you as your everything.

SCRIPTURE

*My sister, my bride, you are
like a garden locked up,
like a walled-in spring,
a closed-up fountain.
Your limbs are like an orchard
of pomegranates with all
the best fruit,
filled with flowers and nard,
nard and saffron, calamus,
and cinnamon,
with trees of incense,
myrrh, and aloes—
all the best spices.*

SONG OF SOLOMON 4:12–14 NCV

*While He was in Bethany, reclining
at the table in the home of Simon
the Leper, a woman came with an
alabaster jar of very expensive
perfume, made of pure nard. She
broke the jar and poured the
perfume on His head.*

MARK 14:3 NIV

*Keep your eyes on Jesus, who both
began and finished this race we're
in. Study how He did it. Because He
never lost sight of where He was
headed—that exhilarating finish in
and with God—He could put up with
anything along the way: Cross, shame,
whatever. And now He's there, in the
place of honor, right alongside God.*

HEBREWS 12:2 THE MESSAGE

P R A Y E R

Jesus, to love You is my heart's greatest delight. I worship You today just as Mary did, anointing You with my sweet-smelling sacrifice. The cost of the perfume is noteworthy, but it doesn't even compare to the sacrifice You made for me. So today I take my alabaster jar, and I completely break it, knowing that none can be saved and poured out at a later time. It's now or never. And I choose now. Help me to know that whatever I choose to bring, it's not about the dollar sign that matters to You; it's about my heart posture. So I turn my heart toward You and tell You that You are more than my Prayer Buddy or even my Friend; You are my everything. Put opportunities in my path this week for me to worship You in an unabashed way. Keep me both humble and bold like Mary was. Thank You for bringing light to my darkness and rescuing me from the pit. For that, I pour out everything that I have onto You, and I will rest in Your goodness. In Your beautiful name, Jesus. Amen.

Moment to Breathe

Take a moment to breathe in God's rest and exhale out your sacrifice. Imagine that you are married to a good man and the two of you have been diligently saving for your retirement. Then one day you call him at work and ask if he would liquidate $50,000 from your joint investments and bring the money home with him. Of course, he is taken aback and asks what the money is for. You tell him that you would like to purchase some pure nard made from rare plants in India so that you can pour it out over Jesus as a sweet-smelling sacrifice. Your husband kindly but directly reminds you how hard you both have worked to save this money. You tell him that you understand his concern, but the cost will be worth it, and besides, the cost doesn't even compare to what Jesus has done for you. You husband has indeed seen the change that Jesus has invoked in you, so he agrees to bring home the money for this very expensive perfume. You thank him and hang up the phone, knowing that there is no better use of your sacrifice than to pour it all out for Jesus. So take a deep breath in and receive your alabaster jar.

Bring your praise as an offering and your thanks as a sacrifice as you sing your story of miracles with a joyful song. PSALM 107:22 TPT

DO IT ANYWAY

Some of those present were saying indignantly to one another, "Why this waste of perfume? It could have been sold for more than a year's wages and the money given to the poor." And they rebuked her harshly. "Leave her alone," said Jesus. "Why are you bothering her? She has done a beautiful thing to Me. The poor you will always have with you, and you can help them any time you want. But you will not always have Me. She did what she could." MARK 14:4–8 NIV

People can be fickle. We can be celebrated one day and crucified the next by the same person. What causes the shift? It could be attributed to false information, or it could actually be due to something we did, intentional or not. But more often than not, pride has a sneaky way of making even the best of people turn on each other.

Mary consistently proved herself to be pure of heart, but that didn't stop the bystanders from turning on her as she extravagantly and intentionally poured her expensive perfume onto Jesus. As this act of love and adoration was taking place, there were a few at the dinner party who were not impressed with her anointing of Jesus. So, what did they do? They started gossiping about her to each other. *"Why this waste of perfume? It could have been sold for more than a year's wages and the money given to the poor."* They finally got each other so worked up over it that they couldn't hold it in any longer. And while she was literally at Jesus's feet, they came up to her and rebuked her harshly—right in front of Jesus's oil-streaked face. What a scene!

But, as a faithful Savior does, Jesus came to her rescue and told these rude bystanders to stop bothering her. Jesus could see their hearts, and He knew they had been stirring the pot, causing dissension among the dinner guests, and at the root of it was pride. It wasn't about the poor. It was about the fact that Mary was doing what they should have been doing, and so they sought to shame her. But Jesus called them on it and said, *"She has done a beautiful thing to Me. The poor you will always have with you, and you can help them any time you want. But you will not always have Me. She did what she could."* Mary did what she could, and it was considered by the Almighty to be a beautiful thing.

We have the same opportunity to do what we can for Jesus in our lives. Will we be misunderstood? It's probable. Will our friends turn on us? Possibly. But should we do it anyway if it brings glory to Him? Always.

If we have a pure heart like Mary did, the truth will shine forth. We don't have to defend or explain ourselves. Jesus will do that for us. Oftentimes, the best thing we can do is stay silent and let Him silence those who have come against us. He knows their hearts as well as He knows ours. We just need to be obedient to do what we can to bring Him glory, knowing that it will be considered by the Almighty as a beautiful thing.

Reflection

- Q U E S T I O N S -

Have you felt undue criticism from others before? Have you ever found yourself in a situation where you've unjustly criticized or judged others? How did you handle it?

_____

_____

_____

_____

_____

_____

_____

_____

_____

_____

_____

_____

_____

_____

_____

_____

_____

_____

_____

_____

We can all think of times when our actions have been driven by a desire for recognition or approval rather than our genuine love for Jesus. Write some ways we could all cultivate a spirit of selfless love and generosity, like Mary's.

_____

_____

_____

_____

_____

_____

_____

_____

Mary was obedient to keep pouring her expensive perfume onto Jesus even though the motives of her heart were being questioned. Has your heart for Jesus ever been misunderstood? Tell of that time. Then record how Jesus views your gift. Were you able to hear Him say that you have done a beautiful thing?

_____

_____

_____

_____

_____

_____

_____

_____

SCRIPTURE

At my first defense, no one came to my support, but everyone deserted me. May it not be held against them. But the Lord stood at my side and gave me strength, so that through me the message might be fully proclaimed and all the Gentiles might hear it. And I was delivered from the lion's mouth. The Lord will rescue me from every evil attack and will bring me safely to His heavenly kingdom. To Him be glory for ever and ever. Amen.

II TIMOTHY 4:16–18 NIV

I, Wisdom, live together with good judgment. I know where to discover knowledge and discernment. All who fear the LORD will hate evil. Therefore, I hate pride and arrogance, corruption and perverse speech.

PROVERBS 8:12–13 NLT

Where there is strife, there is pride, but wisdom is found in those who take advice.

PROVERBS 13:10 NIV

Now the goal of our instruction is love that comes from a pure heart, a good conscience, and a sincere faith.

I TIMOTHY 1:5 CSB

P R A Y E R

Lord, it hurts to have friends misunderstand the motives of my heart. I know You understand this more than anyone. Your friends deserted You and even denied You, yet You forgave them. Give me the ability to do the same for those who have turned on me. Test the motives of my heart and reveal to me if there is any impurity there. If not, then I ask You to come to my defense, just as You did for Mary. You are a faithful Savior, and I resolve to keep my eyes on You and not the bystanders. Receive my gift of love as I seek to give You glory. Don't let my faith waver. Keep me doing it anyway, knowing that You consider my gift to be a beautiful thing. To have the Almighty say such words is what my soul longs to hear. There is simply nothing better, and I rest in that, just as I rest in You today. Thank You for loving me like You do. Amen.

Moment to Breathe

Take a moment to breathe in God's rest and exhale out your hurt and betrayal. Imagine that you are sitting on a park bench watching little children play happily in the sandbox. Then one of them finds a garnet ring buried deep within the sand. Her face is filled with amazement and delight at her discovery. She stands up quickly, eager to take the ring to her Father, but the others playing in the sandbox are jealous that she found something they didn't, so they seek to take it from her. Her Father sees the commotion and comes to the sandbox to inquire of the dispute. The girl shows Him the ring, and He opens His hand to receive it. He says that it is a beautiful ring indeed, fit for royalty. And the little girl knows she has done the right thing in giving the ring to Him. She did what she could. With that in mind, take a deep breath in and receive affirmation from the Almighty that your gift to Him is a beautiful thing.

The LORD your God is with you; the mighty One will save you. He will rejoice over you. You will rest in His love; He will sing and be joyful about you. ZEPHANIAH 3:17 NCV

A WOMAN OF LEGACY

"She did what she could. She poured perfume on My body beforehand to prepare for My burial. Truly I tell you, wherever the gospel is preached throughout the world, what she has done will also be told, in memory of her." Mark 14:8–9 NIV

Legacy. Few words carry such a large connotation. Each one of us will eventually reach the end of our lives and will be remembered for something—either good, bad, or indifferent. But it's those who choose to leave a legacy who will reach into the next generation. They will leave those whom they have touched with something of value, their impact never fully realized in their own eyes on this side of eternity.

Mary was a woman of legacy. She didn't build it by anything she said, but rather she built it with her actions. This woman, who only spoke one recorded sentence in all of Scripture, has been remembered for over two thousand years, and her example will live on forever. That is a direct result of Mary's heart posture—each encounter landing her at the feet of Jesus. She sat at His feet to listen to His teaching. She fell at His feet and presented Him with her grief and pain. She poured out her love onto His feet and wiped them with her long hair. She wasn't trying to be the smartest person in the room or the most talented or the most admired. She simply stayed at His feet.

Because Mary was diligent to stay at Jesus's feet, she did something truly remarkable at the most critical time. You see, Jesus had already told His disciples on three separate occasions that He was to be crucified, but it didn't seem to be sinking in. However, here came Mary with her alabaster jar of very expensive perfume, and she anointed Jesus *before* His burial. The motivation for her actions was love and worship, but the implications were enormous in the spiritual realm. The next few days would prove to be the hardest of Jesus's earthly life, but isn't it thrilling to know that as He endured them, He still smelled like Mary's spikenard? *"Truly I tell you, wherever the gospel is preached throughout the world, what she has done will also be told, in memory of her."* Jesus's words ring true today. Mary left a legacy by placing herself at the feet of Jesus over and over again.

To be a woman of legacy is not about building our fame or fortune. It's not even about how much we talk about Jesus; it's more about how we act like Him. And the only way we are going to act more like Him is to place ourselves at His feet over and over again. At His feet we learn what His Word says about who we are in Him. At His feet is where we fall for healing when we are broken and hurting. At His feet is where we worship Him with every ounce of our being. And as we get up to attend to our business and daily lives, we find that we, too, smell of the expensive perfume of spikenard. It has seeped into our hands and our hair, reminding us to continue to rest in Jesus.

Reflection
- QUESTIONS -

Jesus said that Mary was anointing Him to prepare Him for His upcoming burial. Do you think she was even aware of the significance of her timing, or that she was simply acting in obedience to the prompting of the Holy Spirit? Explain your answer below.

Mary's legacy was directly tied to her willingness to pour out the perfume onto Jesus. Jesus said that wherever the Gospel is preached throughout the world, her memory will stand. How do you consider the Gospel being tied to your legacy? What act of obedience is necessary to build your legacy?

Mary is most remembered not for what she said, but for how she acted. In what ways have you seen this to be true in your own life? How can you be more conscious of how your actions point to Jesus in your everyday life? List an idea or two below.

S C R I P T U R E

Then He called the crowd to Him along with His disciples and said: "Whoever wants to be My disciple must deny themselves and take up their cross and follow Me. For whoever wants to save their life will lose it, but whoever loses their life for Me and for the gospel will save it."

MARK 8:34–35 NIV

He has saved us and called us to a holy life—not because of anything we have done but because of His own purpose and grace. This grace was given us in Christ Jesus before the beginning of time, but it has now been revealed through the appearing of our Savior, Christ Jesus, who has destroyed death and has brought life and immortality to light through the gospel.

II TIMOTHY 1:9–10 NIV

Do everything without grumbling and arguing, so that you may be blameless and pure, children of God who are faultless in a crooked and perverted generation, among whom you shine like stars in the world, by holding firm to the word of life.

PHILIPPIANS 2:14–16 CSB

PRAYER

Dear Lord, it's hard to put into words what I want to say. It's not about me. It never has been. It's all about You. To leave a legacy that is tied to the Gospel is the only thing that will matter once this life is said and done. I don't want to be remembered for the things I said or the things I achieved. I want to be remembered as a woman who loved You with her whole heart and then let that love spill out onto others. Forgive me when I get it backward. Redirect me when I want to take the glory for myself. Encourage me when I act like You would act. Take my life and let it point to You. Let me preach the Gospel with the way I demonstrate the fact that I am a sinful woman who received grace and that same grace is available to all who want it. Make it evident, and may the next generation feel the impact of my legacy because of who You are to me. I love You to eternity. Amen.

Moment to Breathe

Take a moment to breathe in God's rest and exhale out your past. Imagine that you are sitting at a desk as a mature woman writing a letter to your younger self. You start off by telling her to take just a moment to rest in God's love. Her life is hectic, and she is busy running from here to there, but God has so much in store for her if she will take the time to turn to Him first. You also tell her that life is sometimes hard, and there will be valleys she will have to endure, but not to fear, because Jesus will be right there with her the entire time. You insist that she is to let her light shine brightly because it will point others to Jesus, and the best part is that the Father will be glorified when she does good things in her life. You end by affirming her work ethic, but you encourage her to take the time to sit at Jesus's feet, day in and day out, because at His feet is where her legacy lies. Take another deep breath in and receive your Gospel-centered legacy.

Many women do noble things, but you surpass them all. PROVERBS 31:29 NIV

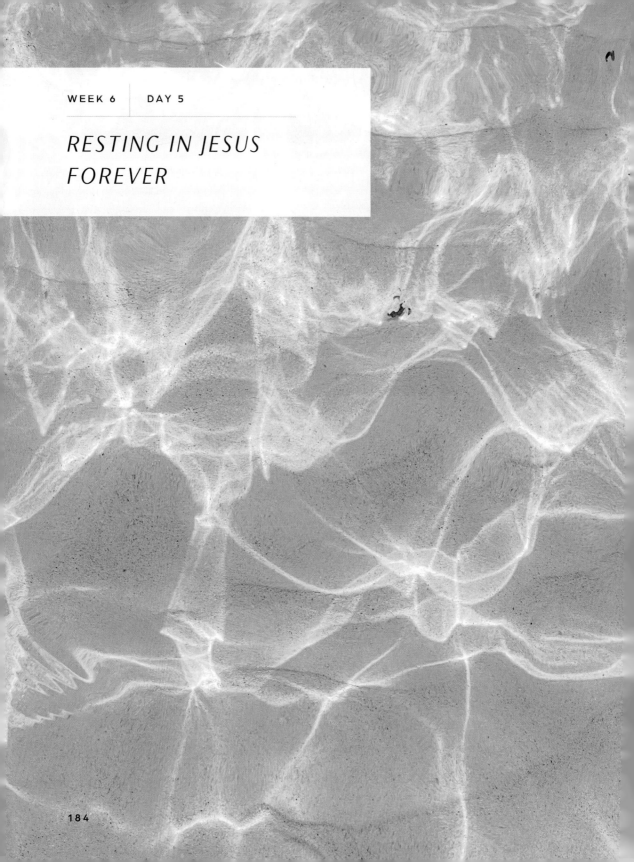

RESTING IN JESUS FOREVER

The LORD is my shepherd; I have what I need. He lets me lie down in green pastures; He leads me beside quiet waters. He renews my life; He leads me along the right paths for His name's sake. Even when I go through the darkest valley, I fear no danger, for You are with me; Your rod and your staff— they comfort me. You prepare a table before me in the presence of my enemies; You anoint my head with oil; my cup overflows. Only goodness and faithful love will pursue me all the days of my life, and I will dwell in the house of the LORD as long as I live. PSALM 23 CSB

Oh, friend! What a bittersweet moment to know that our journey has come to an end. As we linger at the dinner party for a minute longer, let's reminisce about the past as we look forward to the future, resting upon Jesus as we do.

We learned from Martha that in order to rest in Jesus, we must first welcome Him into our hearts and homes. Furthermore, we invite Him into every aspect of our lives, not just relegating Him to one or two spaces. He wants all of us, just as He gave Himself fully to us. He asks that we don't become so distracted with serving everyone else that we miss what is of greater importance—sitting with Him.

Martha also taught us that belief is a big deal to God. He wants us to bring our doubts and fears to Him, but He also wants us to trust that He is who He says He is. He is the Resurrection and the Life, the God who brings dead things to life, but even more than that, He promises us eternal life with Him *if* we believe.

Mary had much to teach us about being pure in heart. She was willing to place herself at the feet of Jesus over and over again and because she did, we are still talking about her all these years later. What made Mary special was both her boldness and humility. She sat when women didn't typically sit at the feet of a rabbi, and not only was she welcomed by Jesus, but she was applauded for making the better choice. She was vulnerable with Jesus about her grief over losing Lazarus, bringing Him her brokenness. And last but not least, she knelt at Jesus's feet to pour out her love and adoration, and in doing so, she left a legacy to last for eternity.

These two sisters gave us an amazing gift in showing us how we can now better view rest—because resting in Jesus has far less to do with taking a break as it does trusting and believing in Him—even when our circumstances are less than ideal or even dire.

The party may be over, but our individual journeys are not. As we continue to walk with purpose, may we never forget where our true rest lies. Jesus is the only One capable of giving us that deep, soul-satisfying rest we crave, but we must be willing to come to Him, believing He is the Son of God. He is trustworthy and the only One worthy of all our honor and praise.

Reflection
- QUESTIONS -

After walking with Mary and Martha these past few weeks, what are some of the highlights you learned from each sister? List how you can implement those lessons into your everyday life from here on out.

_____

_____

_____

_____

_____

_____

_____

_____

_____

_____

_____

_____

_____

_____

_____

_____

_____

_____

If a friend were to approach you and ask what it means to rest in Jesus, what would you say to her?

Turn back to Week 1, Day 1 of this devotional guide and reread your answer to what you hoped to get out of Resting in Jesus. *Do you feel as if your expectations were realized? Why or why not?*

SCRIPTURE

Jesus replied, "Now you finally believe in Me. And the time has come when you will all be scattered, and each one of you will go your own way, leaving Me alone! Yet I am never alone, for the Father is always with Me. And everything I've taught you is so that the peace which is in Me will be in you and will give you great confidence as you rest in Me. For in this unbelieving world you will experience trouble and sorrows, but you must be courageous, for I have conquered the world!"

JOHN 16:31–33 TPT

"As the Father has loved Me, so have I loved you. Now remain in My love. If you keep My commands, you will remain in My love, just as I have kept My Father's commands and remain in His love. I have told you this so that My joy may be in you and that your joy may be complete. My command is this: Love each other as I have loved you. Greater love has no one than this: to lay down one's life for one's friends. You are My friends if you do what I command. I no longer call you servants, because a servant does not know his master's business. Instead, I have called you friends, for everything that I learned from My Father I have made known to you."

JOHN 15:9–15 NIV

And I'm an olive tree,
growing green in God's house.
I trusted in the generous mercy
of God then and now.
I thank You always
that You went into action.
And I'll stay right here,
Your good name my hope,
in company with Your faithful friends.

PSALM 52:8–9 THE MESSAGE

PRAYER

Jesus, Son of God, Light of the World, Resurrection and Life, Teacher, Master, Savior, and Friend, You are the One who brings rest to my weary soul. You bring light to my darkness. You bring purpose to my pain. You bring calm to my chaos. You bring joy to my life. You are not just a God who is on Your throne and is absent from my daily life. No, You are a God who hears me when I call to You. You answer me when I pray. You find pleasure in having a relationship with me. You love me with an unconditional love, and You call me by name. You ask me if I believe in You, and I do wholeheartedly. You weep when I weep and rejoice when I rejoice. You redeemed my life from the pit, and You instruct me to strip off the old labels that are holding me back. When I pour out my love on You, You tell me that I have done a beautiful thing. You give me a legacy because I honor You. Thank You for all that You have given to me through this walk with Mary, Martha, and You. May I never stop resting in You. Amen.

Moment to Breathe

Take a moment to breathe in God's rest and exhale out your completeness, knowing in your heart that you have everything you need. Imagine you are back at the beach, walking along the shoreline as the sun begins to rise. The waves are calm, and the sand is cool beneath your feet. Your soul feels restored because you have been with the Master. He led you down this particular path of life so that He alone would get the glory. Even when times were dark and your pain threatened to swallow you whole, He was with you—comforting you, weeping with you, and redeeming you. He invited you to sit at His feet so He could teach you what it means to follow Him. He filled you to the brim with His soul-satisfying rest and hope because you chose to believe in Him as the Son of God. You know that because of who you are in Him, only goodness and faithful love will pursue you all your days. As you breathe in the salty air one final time, you vow to sit at His feet, trust in His heart, and pour out your love onto Him, resting in Jesus forever.

I see that the LORD is always with me. I will not be shaken, for He is right beside me.
No wonder my heart is glad, and my tongue shouts His praises! My body rests in hope.
ACTS 2:25–26 NLT